BRIGHT NOTES

# BELOVED BY TONI MORRISON

Intelligent Education

INFLUENCE PUBLISHERS

Nashville, Tennessee

BRIGHT NOTES: Beloved
www.BrightNotes.com



ISBN: 978-1-645425-10-6 (Paperback)
ISBN: 978-1-645425-11-3 (eBook)

Published in accordance with the U.S. Copyright Office Orphan Works and Mass Digitization report of the register of copyrights, June 2015.

Originally published by Monarch Press.
Eleanor Branch, 1988
2019 Edition published by Influence Publishers.

Interior design by Lapiz Digital Services. Cover Design by Thinkpen Designs.

Printed in the United States of America.

Library of Congress Cataloging-in-Publication Data forthcoming.
Names: Intelligent Education
Title: BRIGHT NOTES: Beloved
Subject: STU004000 STUDY AIDS / Book Notes

# CONTENTS

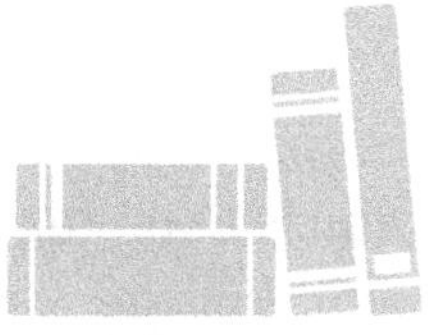

# INTRODUCTION TO TONI MORRISON

## THE EARLY YEARS

Toni Morrison was born Chloe Anthony Wofford in Lorain, Ohio, a steel-mill town on Lake Erie, in 1931. The second of four children, she was a Depression-era baby in a large and close-knit family whose roots stretched deep into the South. Her maternal grandfather was five when he crawled under a bed to hide from the coming "Emancipation Proclamation." As a violinist and carpenter in his adult years, he lived with and often expected the hypocrisy of many white Americans. His wife was an optimist, however. She believed that with faith and action, anything was possible.

Morrison's parents mirrored those philosophies in much the same way. Her father, a native of Georgia and a shipyard worker who held three jobs off and on for 17 years, once threw a white man down the steps. Her mother wrote a letter to the President Franklin Delano Roosevelt complaining of the food quality when the family was forced to go on relief; she got action. Morrison says of her childhood, "I grew up in a basically racist household with more than a child's share of contempt for white people."

Out of that experience came the traditions that exist in her work today. Everywhere in her life there was a reverence for the language and lore, the traditions, myths and rituals of black people. She spent hours listening to the ghost stories her parents would tell. Her grandmother kept a dream book, using it to decipher images and symbols in order to play the numbers. Her mother, a member of the choir, sang constantly. These things find their home in Morrison's fiction.

In high school, she learned Latin and discovered Gustave Flaubert's *Madame Bovary*, Jane Austen's novels, and other great literature, including the Russian novels. Always a good student, she graduated as a member of the National Honor Society, and went on to Howard University in Washington, D.C. She wanted to be a dancer, but recalls that what she did well was read.

## BEYOND OHIO

At Howard, Chloe Anthony became Toni. She also traveled with the university's repertory company, which gave her the opportunity to see firsthand the black South of the late 40s and early 50s. She drew connections as a result of this experience, and the ties to and reverence for her ancestors were cemented further.

After Howard, Morrison attended Cornell University for a Master's Degree in English. Later, she taught briefly at Texas Southern University, returning to Howard as an instructor in 1957. In the dawn of the civil rights struggle, she taught many of the students who would one day be at the forefront of the movement-Stokeley Carmichael, Andrew Young, Leroi Jones (Amiri Baraka), and others. She also joined a writers' group where she began the short story that would later become her first novel, *The Bluest Eye*.

During this period, she also met and married Harold Morrison, a Jamaican architecture student. The marriage lasted six years and in 1964 with one child and one on the way, Morrison found herself divorced. With no prospects of gainful employment, she returned to her parents' home in Lorain. A little more than a year later, she was back on the east coast, having accepted a job in Syracuse, New York, as a textbook editor, with the proviso that she would soon be transferred to the textbook department at Random House in New York City.

Against this backdrop, Morrison began to write seriously. *The Bluest Eye*, published in 1970 to respectable reviews but limited success, was written out of the turmoil of a young woman in a strange place with two children and very few friends. It wasn't long before she was on to New York and Random House.

## BRIGHT LIGHTS, BIG CITY

An editor at Random House for 18 years, Morrison began in the textbook department and was quickly transferred to trade as a consequence of the black cultural awakening of the late 60s-early 70s. Her work-almost exclusively with black writers-included books by Muhammad Ali and black woman authors such as Angela Davis, Toni Cade Bambara, and Gayle Jones. She also worked on The *Black Book*, a compendium of black American life that dates back 300 years, and Ivan Van Sertima's *They Came Before Columbus*.

Between working and raising two sons, Morrison started Sula, her second novel which, she says, was partly composed during her commute from her home in Queens to work in Manhattan. Published in 1973, the book debuted to rave reviews and earned the author national recognition as a talent to watch.

Song of Solomon came four years later to an even warmer reception. A best-seller, it won the National Book Critics Circle Award as well as the American Academy and Institute of Arts and Letters Award for fiction. It was also the first black novel selected to be a Book-of-the-Month-Club offering since Richard Wright's *Native Son* in 1940.

In 1981, among more critical acclaim, Morrison's fourth novel, Tar Baby, appeared, earning its author a spot on the cover of Newsweek magazine. It also became a best-seller. At the time Morrison believed that her writing days were over. "I would not write another novel to either make a living or because I was able to," she told the Wall Street Journal. "If it was not an overwhelming compulsion or I didn't feel absolutely driven by the ideas that I wanted to explore, I wouldn't do it. And I was content not to ever be driven that way again."

Morrison did put her skills to use, however. In 1983, she wrote the book and lyrics for a little known musical called New Orleans and in 1986, her play, Dreaming Emmett, premiered in Albany to mark the first annual celebration of slain civil rights leader Martin Luther King Jr.'s birthday as a national holiday.

## THE SEEDS OF BELOVED

For *Beloved,* Morrison reached back into her editorial experience at Random House and her work on *The Black Book*. From a newspaper clipping contained in that work, she found an idea compelling enough for her to return to the novel form. The article, entitled "A Visit to the Slave Mother Who Killed Her Child," was one account of a reporter's meeting with Margaret Garner, a runaway slave from Kentucky, who in 1855 tried to kill her children rather than face a return to slavery. She succeeded in killing one and it is her story that forms the germ of Morrison's book. It was to be only the beginning, however, as Morrison's intention to create a novel that followed the lives of her slave-turned-free characters and their descendants into the twentieth century became a trilogy. *Beloved* is the first installment.

## CONTROVERSY AND THE PULITZER PRIZE

*Beloved* appeared in 1987 to much critical acclaim. The novel was, by turns, nominated for the National Book Award, the National Book Critics Circle Award, the Ritz-Hemingway Prize in Paris and finally the Pulitzer Prize. As a result of her failure to receive the 1987 National Book Award, a group of 48 black writers published a letter of protest in the New York Times Book Review questioning why such a talented author had not received so prestigious an award as the Book Award or the Pulitzer. It was to become a moot point, for on March 31, 1988, Toni Morrison won the latter. She told the New York Times, "In the end I feel as though I have served the characters in the book well and I have served the readers well and I hope the Pulitzer people are as proud of me as I am of them."

## TONI MORRISON, THE WRITER

Morrison has been cited for the lushness and vitality of her language and challenged for her often brutal exploration of black life. She has also accepted the labeling-black writer, woman writer, black woman writer. She contends that the strength of her writing lies in the language, its oral quality, its ability to draw the reader in and to establish a participatory relationship with him or her.

Morrison, by her own admission, writes "village" or "peasant" literature. Written for black people, it is universal because the stories and themes within touch all who read it. Peasant literature serves an important function in that it is **didactic**, a means of reasserting the rules of survival. In a New Republic interview, Morrison summed it up this way: "I think long and carefully about what my novels ought to do. They should clarify the roles that have become obscured; they ought to identify those things in the past that are useful and those things that are not; and they ought to give nourishment."

To that end, Morrison works with **cliches** and metaphors, milking them until they reflect the very essence on which they are founded and lifting simple truths into the complex reality of our world for all to see.

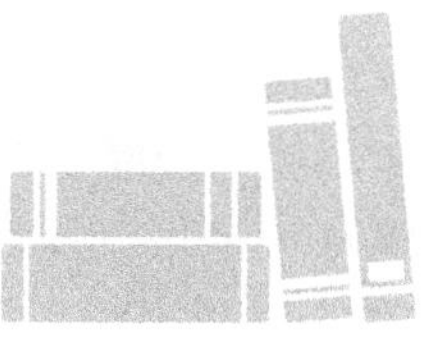

# BELOVED

## INTRODUCTION

No thorough examination of *Beloved* can be initiated without a complete understanding of the story, its plot complexities, and the various thematic and literary devices Morrison uses in the development of her work. What follows is a brief overview of the novel with special consideration given to these areas.

### STORY AND PLOT

Although the story of *Beloved* begins far earlier, the novel opens with the narrator setting the time and place in Cincinnati, 1873. Sethe, a former slave on a Kentucky plantation called Sweet Home, has been free for 18 years. She lives with her 18-year-old daughter, Denver, in a house called 124 that is haunted by the ghost of her dead baby girl. Her sons, frightened away by the unfamiliar, run away early in their adolescence, and her mother-in-law, Baby Suggs, whose residence she sought after her escape from slavery, is dead.

Isolated from the rest of the community, Sethe spends her days, "beating back the past," and is awakened to the possibilities of a future with the arrival of Paul D, also a former Sweet Home slave. He is immediately invited in, exorcises the ghost and attempts to forge a family relationship with Sethe and a recalcitrant Denver.

The ghost, however, returns incarnate to reclaim her family. Arriving one afternoon, with no memory of her past or present, she says her name is Beloved, and is taken in. In a subtle game of dominance, she drives Paul D out of Sethe's bedroom, charms Denver, and slowly begins a kind of parasitic destruction of Sethe.

Throughout the novel, events in real time are interrupted by memory. Sethe and Paul D have just begun to work through painful recollections of slavery when he is told the awful truth: Sethe murdered her baby to protect it from the horrors of slavery. Confronting her, he leaves, and she folds under the weight of her own grief and guilt. Losing interest in the outside world, she becomes mired in an attempt to explain to Beloved the rationale behind her act.

It is not long before Denver realizes the toll Beloved's presence has exacted on Sethe and that she must save her family. She seeks help from the townspeople who, 30-women strong, come to exorcise Beloved with their prayers. Paul D subsequently returns to a psychically wounded Sethe.

## THEMATIC CONSIDERATIONS

Toni Morrison writes from a particular tradition, offering up a forceful vision and poignant evocation of the black American experience. In *Beloved*, she draws a complicated portrait of slavery and its effects on selfhood and motherhood. Using a variety of **themes** and motifs, she creates an often unsettling, yet palpable statement about the "peculiar institution" that so informed the history of the United States.

Morrison herself acknowledges the patterns of cultural tradition and imperative that inform her work. They have become the basis for a prose that is both imagistic and didactic.

To begin, we examine two important and fundamental principles that serve as the foundation to the major action in *Beloved*: the reverence for ancestors and the sense of continuity their presence brings to the lives of the characters and to the work itself; and the absolute acceptance of the supernatural as an integral part of everyday life.

These themes, in combination with others, make *Beloved* an American masterpiece, a richly textured and evocative recreation of a period in this country's history still too painful for many to explore.

## TEN MAJOR THEMES

1. Ancestor-elders provide a sense of continuity in life. They represent connections to the past and are a source of strength and wisdom. Survival is linked to an acceptance of the role they play in our lives.

2. The supernatural is a fact of life. Morrison does not ask us to suspend disbelief, rather to accept the presence-as the characters themselves do-of a different kind of knowledge, one that enhances rather than negates real life experience.

3. Slavery distorts even the most basic of human instincts, like motherhood, and leaves absolutely no room for "personhood."

4. Mother love, that vibrant, intangible expression of love for one's children, can be intensely compelling and highly destructive.

5. A woman's search for self is often an internal quest-a search for meaning and a sense of personal value. This same quest operates differently in men because it is externally-based.

6. Survival depends on the acceptance and integration of what is past and what is present. Memory plays an important role in that it is cathartic.

7. Self-love and self-possession are necessary tools for survival.

8. The community responds to people and events as a living, breathing organism with all the human tendencies to nurture and support on the one hand and to be mean and vindictive on the other.

9. Isolation from family, community, and self is devastating to the human spirit.

10. The ability to reconcile and to experience redemption are functions of personal growth.

A series of motifs, recurring thematic elements that support the major issues of the novel, will also be examined in the textual analysis of theme. Counted among them are defeat, obsession, abandonment, and the cycle of birth, death, and rebirth.

A discussion of the literary techniques Morrison uses to accomplish her thematic goals follows.

## PLOT STRUCTURE

In pursuing an intense psychological inquiry into the nature of slavery and its effect on the slave, Morrison uses suspense to pull us into the story and personal involvement with the characters. Immediately we know there is a secret-a child that has died and returned to haunt its mother. The particulars are not known-the how or the why, but in a series of flashbacks and through the use of **foreshadowing**, we learn little by little, until more than halfway through the novel we are finally told what happened. The why comes to us gradually as a reflection of the trauma slavery has wrought in the minds of the major characters; Morrison paints a psychological portrait of people trying to "forget" something that is unforgettable because forgetting means survival. We are constantly reminded of the horror that slavery was and asked to question the inevitability of the decision Sethe makes.

## REALISM

**Realism**, as a kind of photographic recording or description of events, is part and parcel of the *Beloved* saga. Balanced by the surreal intrusion of memory, the novel's realistic tenor brings into focus the kind of life available to black people as both freemen and slaves in the latter half of the 19th century. How one goes about the business of living after an experience that negates the concept of self is the focal concern.

## SURREALISM

Morrison tackles surrealism, the practice of producing fantastic or incongruous **imagery** or effects, on a number of levels. The movement of characters in and out of their memories helps to give the book its haunting or nightmarish edge. These memories, juxtaposed against images or events that would otherwise seem harmless, are not always triggered by conscious stimuli.

In later chapters, Morrison uses surrealism to develop the obsessional and otherworldly qualities of Beloved. The writing here is in marked contrast to the rest of the book, and Morrison uses it to zero in on the struggle between Beloved and Sethe.

## LYRICAL PROSE STYLE

The oral quality of Morrison's work is supported by her use of language. The **diction** is strong, the images rich, and the **syntax** incredibly varied. Repetition creates emphasis and the marked use of **assonance** (repetition of vowel sounds), and to a lesser degree, **alliteration** (repetition of initial consonant sounds), helps to give the work its sensuousness. In scenes that are rooted in more surreal terms, especially those having to do with *Beloved*, there is a noted contrast. The wordplay is in short staccato bursts. The sentences are more stream-of-consciousness and there is little or no punctuation.

## POINT OF VIEW

One of the most important techniques available to an author in determining how finely crafted the characters are is point of view; stories are told in either first person (I, we) or third person (he, she, they). In first person, the insights we receive about the world of the novel-story are centered on one character. In third person, the author removes him- or herself, using his or her role as storyteller to highlight the qualities of character and action that he or she deems most important. Within any given novel, point of view may vary. In third person, for example, the author can exercise a great deal of discretion as to what we see and how we see it, using either a limited or omniscient voice. If the author concentrates on the view of one character, he or she is using a "limited" point of view; if the author stands above the work, focusing and refocusing our interest on a number of characters and actions, then he or she is using an "omniscient" voice.

To advance the psychological underpinnings of the novel, Morrison uses an omniscient narrator without giving up certain aspects of the limited voice. Because memories pervade so much of Beloved, we are given the opportunity to settle briefly into one character's inner makeup-his or her thoughts, feelings, personal history, etc.-and then another. Often, we find the jump from one to the next immediate. Morrison uses this to create contrast among the characters.

In four later chapters, the first person is used to highlight the psychological and familial connections created and distorted by the return of Beloved. All of the voices-Sethe's, Denver's, and Beloved's-are given sway in individual chapters and come through as stream of consciousness. In Sethe's case, a kind of monologue informs the stream as she endeavors to explain why she had no choice but to kill her baby.

## SETTING

Although the novel jumps back and forth in time, we know very early on that it is 1873 on the outskirts of Cincinnati. The Emancipation Proclamation, the document signed by President Abraham Lincoln freeing the slaves, is 10 years old. The Civil War has been over for eight years and throughout the country there is a steady rise in Jim Crowism, a philosophy and way of life that advocates segregation of the races.

Ohio is a familiar setting for Morrison. Also an important one historically because it merges the post-Civil War attitudes of the North and South. For many, the Ohio River meant freedom-the northern part of the state playing a prominent role in the underground railroad, the system by which many blacks escaped from slavery. Blacks came north to Ohio for jobs in the plants and mills and a taste of the good life. Others moved on to Canada. The southern portion of the state, however, was less obliging-lynchings and cross-burnings occurred on a regular basis.

## CHARACTERIZATION

Characterization is a basic part of any novel's design. It is what helps us understand, respond, even like or dislike a particular character. It is, in fact, what makes that character a "character." Authors have a variety of ways to draw a character. Many use action as a primary vehicle but there are other ways-description of physical appearance or mannerisms; contrast to other characters; narration or **exposition**; and representation of moments of truth or confession, self-discovery, motivation, and conflict. Even the use of character tags, which isolate a dominant quality of a character and repeat it, reveals something the writer wants the reader to know. Stamp Paid and Schoolteacher are tag names that represent certain traits each man possesses.

Using these techniques the novelist can choose to create characters that are static or dynamic-will they or won't they change?-and round or flat. Round characters are highly developed with a complex set of feelings and attitudes, qualities and flaws. Characters like these come to life for us when we read. They are well-developed and usually function as principals. Flat characters, on the other hand, are one-dimensional. They are often "types," personifications or symbols of some larger issue explored in the work. In *Beloved,* for example, there are community and ancestral voices that take on aspects of character in the sense that they are ubiquitous and represent a chorus of themes.

For Sethe, Paul D, Denver, and Baby Suggs, characterization is drawn complexly; less so for Beloved, Stamp Paid, Schoolteacher, and Ella, and even less so for Mr. and Mrs. Garner and Janey Wagon. Nevertheless, the focus-beyond what impact slavery has had on the lives of former slaves-is on the characters' reaction to Sethe's infanticide 18 years before the novel begins and later to her gradual enslavement by the one known only as Beloved. These reactions form the basis for a series of motifs that dominate the book.

## SYMBOLISM

Because of the clear psychological tenor of *Beloved,* symbolism plays a prominent role in the development of its **theme**.

Symbols, as a means of suggesting or revealing issues that seem impalpable, crowd the narrative, connecting the thematic patterns that Morrison has woven into the work. The character Beloved is the most complex of these symbols, representing on the one hand a physical manifestation and reminder of Sethe's painful decision to murder, and on the other, an opportunity for redemption.

A bridge to the other side, Beloved also represents the ancestors, the 60 million Africans who died in the middle passage. There are other symbols as well, connections really, that tie together the human issues of life and death, "selfhood" and survival. These will be discussed as they present themselves within the work.

## IRONY

**Irony** as incongruity, the difference between what happens and what is expected to happen, between appearance and reality, operates on several levels in *Beloved*. It is most often dramatic **irony**; i.e., we, as readers, see more clearly the ramifications of a particular situation than the characters inside it. For example, we are told very early on that Sethe's experience with slavery is out of the ordinary; that, in fact, her expectations are not realistic. Sethe believes her marriage and family will stay intact, in clear contradiction to both Baby Suggs' and Halle's experiences. We as readers see this; Sethe does not. Morrison says: "A bigger fool never lived."

There are also instances of verbal **irony** (sarcasm) in the work. However, the greatest **irony** is a tragic extension of the dramatic-Sethe, out of an abiding love for her child and an unwillingness to see it exposed to the horrors of slavery, kills it.

## METAPHOR AND SIMILE

The lushness of Morrison's language and her use of **imagery** that appeals to the senses make her writing a harvest of **metaphors** and similes. A metaphor compares two dissimilar things, using highly figurative language, without the words like or as. A **simile**, on the other hand, is also a comparison, but uses the words like or as in a direct equation. For example, Morrison uses the **metaphor** of a restless antelope to describe the effect continuous walking has had on Sethe's unborn baby, and another in the identification of life and death as female and male, respectively, in Paul's prison memories. These are very strong metaphors, strong because of the context in which they exist and what they tell us about the psyche of the characters.

When Morrison talks about the joy shared by Denver, Sethe, and Beloved one night ice skating, she is much softer and her comparison is in simile form: "Their skirts flew like wings and their skin turned pewter in the cold and dying light."

Such language appeals to the senses. Morrison makes us see it and feel it in an attempt to bring the images home, to make them larger than life.

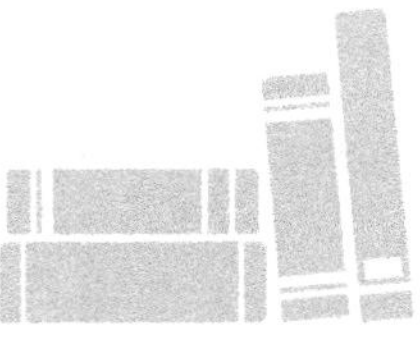

# BELOVED

## TEXTUAL ANALYSIS

## CHAPTER ONE

I Will Call Them My People, Which Were Not My People; And Her *Beloved*, Which Was Not *Beloved*. (Romans 9:25)

An epigraph is a quotation set at the beginning of a literary work that often suggests a **theme**. Morrison's choice is from the New Testament in a chapter where the Apostle Paul voices his concerns about the destiny of his people and the nature of God's interaction with man. The quotation, and its relationship to the novel, can only be understood when taken in the context of the biblical text. Paul's feelings, begun in lament, grow hopeful in the absolute power and mercy of God. The verse immediately following Morrison's chosen quotation heralds reconciliation: "And it shall come to pass, that in the place where it was said unto them, Ye are not my people; there shall they be called the children of the living God." Likewise, later verses proclaim a redemption. As we shall see, these are major **themes** in *Beloved*.

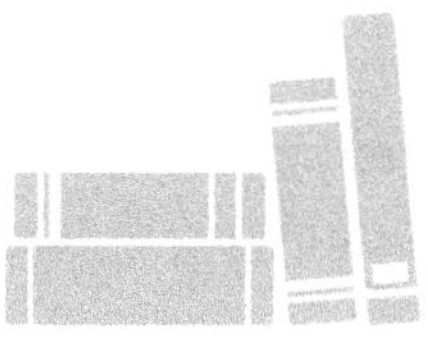

# BELOVED

## TEXTUAL ANALYSIS

## CHAPTER TWO: 124 WAS SPITEFUL

The early chapters of a novel are often devoted to **exposition** or information the author provides us as background to the rest of the story. We are introduced to characters, conflicts, and **themes** that will be developed later. Many authors pique our interest by revealing certain aspects of the story that make us want to read more. One of the ways Morrison does this is to foreshadow something mysterious about the baby's death.

### STRUCTURE

The novel begins in medias res (in the middle of a narrative). The haunting, the death of Baby Suggs, the departure of the boy children are old news. As the novel progresses, a consistent use of flashbacks will not only create a sense of continuity with the past, but develop **exposition** and characterization as well.

Morrison also uses memory to foreshadow future events, as when Sethe and Denver demand that the ghost come forward.

To pique our interest, the first turning point in the novel is also in the first chapter-Paul D exorcises the ghost.

## SETTING

While we know from the first page on that it is 1873 on the outskirts of Cincinnati, the most important piece of information we are furnished with regard to the setting is that it's a house on Bluestone Road called 124. This is very important, so important that Morrison has seen fit to begin the novel with the sentence, "124 was spiteful." Such personification gives the house character and us a sense that a world-the world of the novel-exists primarily within.

## CHARACTERIZATION

This is an important chapter in the characterization of Sethe. She is stoic, even in Denver's eyes, because despite whatever tragedy, she is "one who never looked away." Yet, her weariness is palpable and there is something within her that will ultimately welcome the tyranny of the ghost incarnate.

Note Sethe's reaction to her graveyard barter: "... But those ten minutes she spent pressed up against dawn-colored stone studded with star chips ... were longer than life, more alive, more pulsating than the baby blood that soaked her fingers like oil." Clearly, there is more here than we can see presently if the accoutrements of death are more alive than life itself.

The other characters introduced - Baby Suggs, Paul D, and Denver - are given various treatments. Baby Suggs, by virtue of her age, is ancestor-elder. She too is stoic, defeated finally by her own pain. Paul D seems chameleon-like, changing and adapting to fit the situation; and Denver is victim, a lonely and unhappy adolescent still devastated by the departure of her brothers and the death of her grandmother.

An important moment of clarification in character for both Sethe and Paul D comes in their discussion of the tree on her back and how it got there. Sethe puts the emphasis on the fact that her milk was stolen, Paul D on the fact that they beat her while she was pregnant. This difference in perception reveals two ways of looking at the world and will recur in their quest to forge a solid relationship.

## THEME

Through the process of **exposition**, Morrison acquaints us with some of the **themes** and motifs that she will continue to develop throughout the novel. One of the first to be addressed, and the dominant **theme** throughout, is the existence of the supernatural; 124 is spiteful because a baby ghost lurks there.

Another controlling **theme** is the impact slavery has had on the characters' lives. From Baby Suggs, who remembers very little about her eight children, we learn that the institution of slavery has a debilitating effect on the concept of motherhood and the sense of family; from Sethe, there is a great sense of awe and dread.

Other **themes** are interrelated, e.g., isolation: Sethe and Denver are isolated, in part, because the townspeople won't come near their haunted house. Defeat: Baby Suggs accepts defeat and spends the rest of her life pondering color "suspended between the nastiness of life and the meanness of death." Victimization: Sethe is victim, not only because she barters 10 minutes of sex to get the name "Beloved" printed on a headstone, but because she must face the daily rage of her dead baby, who is the ultimate victim. Redemption comes at the hands of Paul D, whom Sethe allows to take "responsibility for her breasts."

## REALISM

Sethe's mention of the woman in the wagon to whom she gave the responsibility of her children is a subtle reference to the underground railroad. Thousands of blacks escaped the oppression of slavery literally by following the North Star. Along the way, they were aided by black and white men and women who showed them the way, offered them food and lodging or transported them to the next station stop.

## SYMBOLISM

Two important symbols emerge in this chapter: the milk and the tree. The milk, as nourishment, symbolizes the indelible bond between mother and child; the chokecherry tree on Sethe's back is a symbol of resistance and strength, despite life's bitter fruit.

Also symbolic is Paul D's fascination with Sethe's eyes. The idea of vision will be used to support the juxtaposition of their experiences within slavery. The differences, directly related to their sex, are an important point of contrast.

## IRONY

Sethe's memories of life at Sweet Home are far from pleasant. Even the plantation's name is ironic. What she does remember about the place is its beauty-and this feeds the **irony**: "It never looked as terrible as it was," she thinks, "and it made her wonder if hell was a pretty place too."

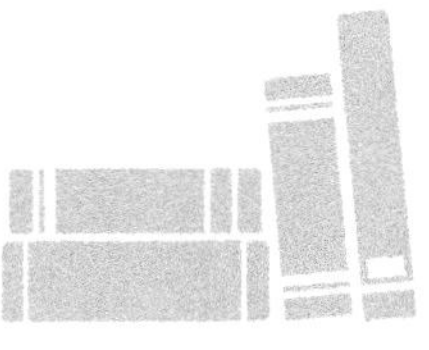

# BELOVED

## TEXTUAL ANALYSIS

## CHAPTER THREE: NOT QUITE IN A HURRY ...

### STRUCTURE

There is a steady movement in this chapter from isolation to connection. Morrison uses the voices of two people, lost from each other in remembrance, and masterfully brings them together by juxtaposing memory against memory until finally their recollections converge on the same episode.

### CHARACTERIZATION

The characterization of Paul D and Sethe is extended further. This comes principally through the intrusion of memory as both characters use the time after sex to reflect on their shared experience of slavery at Sweet Home. Against this backdrop, both struggle to tackle their feelings of inadequacy. Most important, however, we begin to see how Sethe's expectations and perceptions about slavery were naive, even foolish. Sethe's attempt to take possession of herself and her work by bringing things into the kitchen while she worked, and her willingness to take her family for granted, are untenable attitudes for a slave, and Morrison's authorial voice comments strongly: "A bigger fool never lived."

Paul D's retrospection is clouded by his struggle to define himself in relationship to Sixo, another slave on the Sweet Home plantation. Sixo's brand of fiery determination, his boldness and knowingness, become the yardstick by which Paul D measures his own manhood. Not surprisingly, he does not measure up.

## THEME

Motherhood, "familyhood," "personhood" as manifested by slaves become important motifs that support the exploration of slavery and its impact on the slave. Baby Suggs, whose children are taken away one by one, refuses to love any of them, save Halle. Halle, she feels, is a person, a "somebody" because of that connection, that love.

Sethe, whose beliefs are tempered by her own experience, attempts motherhood, familyhood, and personhood in a system that denies the slave these impulses. This is only one of the contradictions that Sethe must face, and her response to it is at the heart of the novel.

## METAPHOR

The sense of desire and sexual gratification is captured in a graceful **metaphor** as Morrison fastens on the images of "loose silk" and "jailed down juice." The corn feast is the **climax** of a year in which the men abused cows while they waited for Sethe to choose a husband.

## IRONY

What should be a moment of tender passion is over too soon and Paul D is left contemplating the **irony** of an 18-year expectation that did not measure up to its reality.

## DENVER'S SECRETS WERE SWEET

### CHARACTERIZATION

The characterization of Denver, Sethe, and Paul D continues through the use of flashbacks, especially Denver's. By juxtaposing memory with scenes from the present, Morrison offers a better understanding of the teenager and her reaction to Paul D. Lonely and troubled, she finds solace inside her own small world and connection in the memories her mother has shared with her regarding her birth. This is one way Denver feeds her hunger. The others are perfume and the boxwood arbor.

But it is also the baby ghost that keeps Denver going, lending an air of excitement to her life. The ghost's departure leaves her that much more lonely and she digs her heels in as a way to punish her mother. In this chapter, we also learn that Denver is a "charmed" child.

Taking another look at Paul D and Sethe, we see two people who are open to the possibilities of a relationship. Sethe, for the first time in almost 18 years, dares to think about what having a life means. However, both are still haunted by the past, still tied to it. Sethe tells Denver that nothing ever dies and vows to keep her from the past, while Paul D fights off his own thoughts about Alfred, Georgia, and jail.

Two other characters are introduced here-Amy Denver, the white girl who helps Sethe deliver Denver, and Schoolteacher. Both are minor characters, with Schoolteacher's name used to tag many of his personality traits.

## THEME

Principal among the many **themes** and motifs that this chapter examines is that of defeat. Where Denver's defeat lies in her isolation, now exacerbated by the absence of the baby ghost, Sethe's defeat begins 18 years before on the banks of the Ohio River when she fears she is dying, and comes back later in her resignation over the baby ghost's tyranny and her belief that making plans is pointless. She is joined by Paul D, who has internalized his defeat by simply shutting down the functions of his brain that are not motor-related.

Morrison hints, too, at the **theme** of mother-daughter conflict as Denver strives to connect with Sethe through a reenactment of the details of her birth, and as Sethe's vague connection with her own "ma'am" comes back to haunt.

The idea of quest is also picked up in Amy's search for velvet, which becomes a **metaphor** for a better life, and Paul D's search for himself and true freedom. Even Sethe is on a quest, although hers is far from external.

Finally, Morrison explores redemption as both Sethe and Paul D begin to see the possibilities open to them.

## METAPHOR

The image of the white dress with its arm around Sethe is a controlling one. Although out of memory, it is taken as an omen by both Sethe and Denver and becomes one of us as well. We expect something to happen, although not necessarily the good things Sethe hopes for.

Another set of images exists in Denver's recounting of her birth. The animal **imagery**, i.e., the antelope and the snake, speaks to certain primitive instincts. Sethe equates the baby kicking inside of her with a restless antelope and later to the dance of her elders when she was young. She imagines herself to be a snake, crawling in the underbrush all "jaws and hunger." What she is creating in her head, however, are images of life, when all her thoughts are of death.

## IRONY

Sethe's description of the manners of Schoolteacher and the nephews is steeped in **irony**. The **allusion** to their stiff formality and gentleness is negated time and time again by acts of violence perpetrated against the slaves at Sweet Home.

## SENSE STIMULI

In what will be a recurring device indicative of conflict, Morrison uses the senses-sight, sound, taste, touch, and smell-to reveal the degree to which a character is open to and interactive with the world around him or her. Sethe's senses are opened with the coming of Paul D. She notices color for the first time since the baby's death: "Things became what they were: drabness looked drab; heat was hot. Windows suddenly had view."

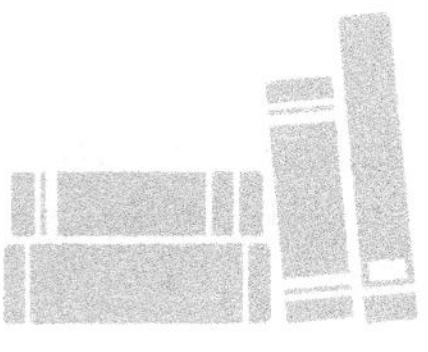

# BELOVED

## TEXTUAL ANALYSIS

## CHAPTER FOUR: PLEASANTLY TROUBLED ...

### STRUCTURE

The story line is anchored in the present as Morrison sets up a picture of family life that will act as a contrast in subsequent chapters.

### CHARACTERIZATION

Denver emerges as a recalcitrant child. Her anger and jealousy finally find direct expression as she confronts Paul D about his intentions toward her mother. Paul D's kindness, however, is contagious and after a day at the carnival, we are hopeful that Denver will soften her attitude.

Sethe, like Denver, is also blossoming; her concern about facing the community and her worry over how she will be perceived is quite telling. Sethe is changing and it is all because of Paul D.

## THEME

The question of how wise it is for an ex-slave mother to invest so much love in her children becomes the focal point. Paul D believes it is risky; Sethe, that it is normal. Both sides are argued briefly, and the dispute ends in a temporary truce. This issue is at the heart of the novel, for Sethe's maternal love, so distorted by the experience of slavery, is the driving force in her life.

## SYMBOLISM

Two images signal conflicting perspectives. The first is the shadow of three people holding hands, a symbol of the possibilities inherent in the family life being developed by Denver, Sethe, and Paul D; and the second, the doomed roses, as an omen of defeat. The fact that both are associated with the carnival is very important because we are at a crossroads in the story. The possibility exists that the threesome could become a family, but as we shall see in the next chapter, the seeds of disruption have already been sown.

## IRONY

The carnival, despite its false promises and perverse people, is enjoyed by the townspeople. The numerous insults are turned around in the "spectacle of whitefolks making a spectacle of themselves."

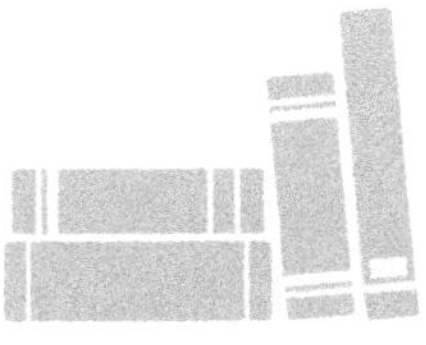



# TEXTUAL ANALYSIS

## CHAPTER FIVE: A FULLY DRESSED WOMAN ...

### STRUCTURE

Beloved's arrival is another turning point in the novel because it upsets the family dynamic that has already begun to develop between Sethe, Denver, and Paul D. A stranger, Beloved is accepted without reservation. Sethe is touched by her name, Paul D wonders about her new shoes, and Denver is delighted. The differences in their reactions provide an excellent opportunity for further characterization using contrast.

### CHARACTERIZATION

The mystery of Beloved is an important part of her characterization. Is she Sethe's daughter returned from the dead or just a stranger in dire need of kindness and a place to stay? We suspect, as Denver does, that this is no ordinary woman; that Beloved could in fact be a reincarnation of Sethe's murdered baby. We know that she walked out of the water; that her skin is lineless and new; that she is incontinent (as any baby might be); that she is taken with color; that she is approximately 19 or 20 (just the age Sethe's child would have been); and that she loves sugar, a detail Morrison alludes to when Sethe places her children on the underground railroad and instructs the "conductor" to nurse the baby with a cloth dipped in sugar water.

Still, Denver's almost voracious devotion to Beloved is a clear indication of how far her loneliness has taken over. More important, however, is Denver's belief that Beloved maybe her sister come back from the dead. If we accept the notion that Denver is a charmed child, then her attention to Beloved, while fed steadily by the hunger of loneliness, comes out of a different kind of knowledge. How else can we explain Denver's certainty that Here Boy won't be coming back?

Paul D and Sethe are divided once again on the issue of nurturing as evidenced by their different reactions to Beloved. Sethe responds as a mother, immediately caring; Paul D is silent, but skeptical. Later his feelings explode as he questions Sethe about her intentions regarding Beloved. Here, Morrison emphasizes the difference in their attitudes. It will come up again and again.

Beyond that, we are called to make a decision with regard to the supernatural. It is not possible to argue that Beloved is simply a manifestation of Sethe's own guilt at having killed her child because both Paul D and Denver see her. Yet, we know that she is no ordinary person. Do we accept Beloved as a ghost incarnate? Denver feels it, but cannot articulate it yet, and much later Sethe, Paul D, and the rest of the community do. In fact, Morrison demands that we do, and in subsequent chapters builds a case to support it.

## SYMBOL

Beloved's association with water is extremely important and is connected to other water **imagery** in the chapter. She walks out of water and upon seeing her, Sethe's urge to urinate is compared to a woman's breaking water in the process of birth. There is also Beloved's unquenchable thirst and her incontinence. The links are drawn clearly. Water itself is a symbol of life, of birth, and Beloved's arrival and placement in the midst of water **imagery** is part of the life-death-rebirth motif that informs the novel.

## THEME

With Beloved's arrival, the supernatural is accentuated, and with it a kind of mystical reverence for water as a symbol of life, death, and rebirth. Since she has lived and died, her rebirth is literally a second chance at life. Her constant association with water as a symbol of life supports this motif. As the story progresses we will see the application of this motif elsewhere.

## REALISM

Morrison paints a picture of post-Civil War life that was disjointed for many black people. Separated from family, faced with the loss of their land or the death of their crops, they wandered in search of a better life and some sort of connection to family and/or community.

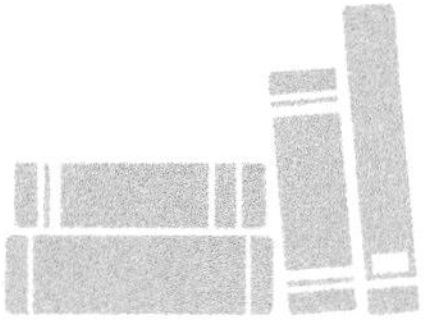

# BELOVED

## TEXTUAL ANALYSIS

## CHAPTER SIX: RAINWATER HELD ON ...

### STRUCTURE

This chapter offers us clue after clue to the identity of Beloved. The questions that she asks Sethe are based on information she could not possibly know if she were a stranger. Denver, who in the last chapter responded almost instinctively to Beloved as her sister, begins to articulate that. The chapter ends in the one question we are asking ourselves: How did Beloved know about the earrings?

Beloved's questions are triggering mechanisms for Sethe. They are an opportunity for her to confront her past without feeling threatened by the memory. It is a brief example of free association-one memory triggering another-in an effort to discover what lies deep inside.

## CHARACTERIZATION

Very little is known about Beloved, only that she seems incredibly devoted to Sethe. It is a devotion that borders on obsession. Beloved cannot take her eyes off Sethe: She follows her around, waits for her to come down in the morning and walks to meet her on the way home at night.

Sethe, flattered by the attention, opens up. Her willingness to relive her memories, her pleasure in the retelling and the acknowledgment (to herself) that some of them are painfully inexplicable-like the memory of Nan and the language she would never know-signify movement in her ability to come to terms with the past. This is an important step in her growth as a human being.

The emphasis is on Beloved, however, and Morrison makes a point of emphasizing the fact that she is different. First, in voice: "They still had not got used to the gravelly voice and the song that seemed to lie in it. Just outside music it lay with a cadence not like theirs." Then in language: Her first question, "Your woman never fix up your hair?" has to be interpreted by Sethe. Woman means mother.

Also in this chapter, Denver's self-absorption is given further sway in her hatred of the stories her mother tells and her wish for Beloved to hate them, too.

## THEME

Obsession becomes a motif as Beloved begins her slow captivation of Sethe. Closely connected with this movement is the **theme** of mother-daughter conflict. Sethe's memory settles on something she recalls about her mother and therefore her past. Beloved's questions are designed to make those connections, and they come out of a need to understand and reconcile the past with the present. Memory, thus, becomes cathartic.

We shall see later on that a resolution of the mother-daughter conflict cannot occur without some reconciliation with the past.

## REALISM

The structure of plantation life for many blacks during slavery is the major point of historical detail addressed in this chapter. We learn: (1) that while slave marriages had no standing in law, the commitment between two people was no less valid than had the marriages been sanctioned legally; (2) that work in the fields extended for long periods of time, even at night if the moon were high; (3) that slaves lived in community settings, and because of the requirements of work, responsibilities like nursing and childcare were distributed to others; and (4) that black women were often sexually exploited by white men, and the products of these unions sometimes faced an ostracism from the rest of the slave community.

We also learn that the slaves were treated like animals and often branded.

## SIMILE

Two very telling **similes** used in the first paragraph seem to explain or foreshadow certain elements in the novel. The first is a comparison of Beloved to a familiar spirit or demon hovering around Sethe. The second is the image of their shadows "clashed and crossed on the ceiling like black swords." Clearly, Morrison is weaving within the text the threads of mystery and suspense that keep us reading. It is wordplay at its finest.

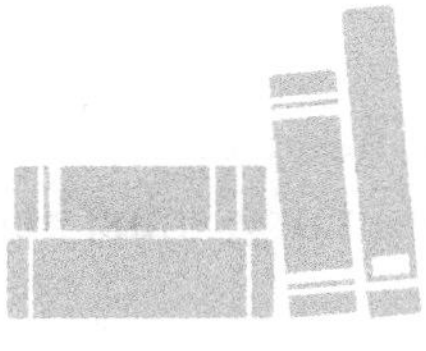

# BELOVED

## TEXTUAL ANALYSIS

## CHAPTER SEVEN: BELOVED WAS SHINING ...

### STRUCTURE

The story continues with Paul D's reaction to the fact that Beloved's presence bodes ill. Characteristically, Morrison dates the movement: it has been five weeks since Beloved's arrival, and the battle lines are firmly drawn. We are also handed several more clues in the mystery of Beloved's identity.

### CHARACTERIZATION

In this chapter, our focus returns to Paul D. Initially skeptical, he is feeling more and more uncomfortable with Beloved's presence, although there remains some question as to why. Is it her sexuality or simply her intrusion on what was an emerging sense of family? Paul D's uncertainty is an important aspect of character, exacerbating his feelings of inadequacy and powerlessness. Never is this more clear than in his recollection of the day Sethe escaped, Halle went crazy and Schoolteacher put a bit in his mouth. Constantly comparing himself without other people and other things, Paul D relates that those events broke him; he felt less a man than Sweet Home's tough barnyard rooster, Mister.

Sethe's reaction to Paul D's confession is important because it challenges the assumptions she has made about Halle, about her life and her future. Made frantic by the relentlessness of her own memories and pain, she is called upon to be supportive of Paul D as he attempts to work through his turmoil. It is too much for both of them, however, and they slip back into an implicit agreement to keep the past at bay.

Also, we are reminded once again how different Beloved is, this time from the perspective of Paul D. The difference disturbs him, yet he is powerless to demand that Sethe throw the young woman out or find her another place to live.

Meanwhile, Denver's attachment to and need for Beloved is growing by leaps and bounds. She takes the opportunity provided by the choking incident to have Beloved sleep with her.

## THEME

The consistent images of defeat make for an overpowering indictment of slavery and what it does to the individual. Sethe and Paul D are beaten back by their memories, defeated as much by the actual circumstances as the emotions their recollections produce.

## REALISM

Slavery, as a system of tyranny and economic exploitation, deprived people of their personhood. The memories Sethe and Paul D must face have everything to do with their treatment as animals, rather than human beings. Sethe is milked like a cow, while Paul D is harnessed as though he were a beast of burden. Morrison continues to fill the novel with an unforgettable picture of what slavery was really like. References to the Ku Klux Klan and their open hostility toward blacks, as well as the sense of urgency and flight that many blacks faced during the period after the Civil War are further examples of realistic detail.

## SYMBOLISM

Paul D's tobacco tin has taken the place of his red heart. The tin is significant because it merges elements of the past with the present. Paul D's tin has not replaced his heart, however; it merely covers it up.

## METAPHOR

Two important **metaphors** dominate this chapter, both having to do with Paul D. The first is his comparison of Beloved to a strawberry plant. The significance here is sexual in nature. Paul D perceives her as "shining," or ripe.

The second is his self-comparison to the rooster, Mister. Roosters are male birds, usually dominant barnyard animals, and Mister is no exception. Even his name tells us what he is and how he is perceived. For Paul D, Mister becomes a symbol of manhood, an intangible that Paul D loses while under the bit.

Other **metaphors** include Paul D's comparison of Beloved to a slippery fish; the Klan as a dragon that swam the Ohio River; and the sticky spider webs that Sethe and Denver emit as a wall of defense against Paul D's dislike of Beloved.

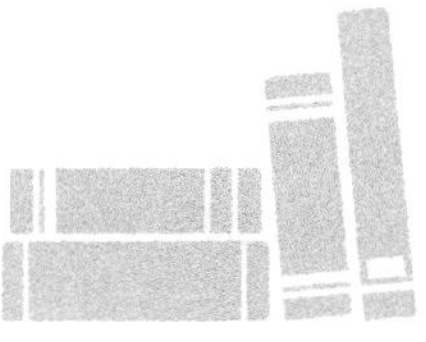

# BELOVED

## TEXTUAL ANALYSIS

## CHAPTER EIGHT: UPSTAIRS BELOVED WAS DANCING

### STRUCTURE

In direct contrast to the previous scene, Beloved and Denver are celebrating. These young women exist in a world all their own, untouched by the tragedy of slavery. It instills in them an abandon neither Sethe nor Paul D has. They are free enough to imagine what it must have been like for Sethe, pregnant and on the run, without any real knowledge of what she was running from. That recollection becomes an echo of their thoughts.

### CHARACTERIZATION

Slowly the level of Beloved's obsession with Sethe is revealed: "She is the one. She is the one I need." Likewise is Denver's desperation over losing Beloved. There is a parallel in their relationships. As devoted as Denver is to Beloved, so Beloved is to Sethe. This will be an important point of contrast as the novel continues.

We also meet Amy Denver again. This time, however, her character is drawn more fully. As a white person, she echoes many of the prejudices whites had toward blacks, yet she is full of kindness. We see her humor and genuine good naturedness, but because the role she plays is so small, we are not privy to any significant character development.

### THEME

Denver's growing obsession with Beloved mirrors Beloved's growing obsession with Sethe, the former exacerbated because Denver finally realizes who Beloved is.

### REALISM

Another parallel that Morrison attempts is the treatment of slaves and indentured servants. Amy is one such servant. She, too, has been beaten; has had to work hours on end; and she faces the possibility of uncertain parentage. Her experience mirrors that of thousands of indentured servants who migrated to America for a better life and who were contracted to work for a set period of time.

### METAPHOR

The tree on Sethe's back returns as a symbol of Sethe's endurance. The water returns along with its associations of life and now freedom as Sethe looks toward the Ohio River and a new life on the other side. The strongest **metaphor**, however, is that of the spores of blue fern lying at the river's edge that come to represent the seeds of the future. A parallel is drawn between the birth of Denver and the potential in those seeds.

## ALLUSION

"The tip of the thing she [Denver] always saw in its entirety when Beloved undressed to sleep" is a subtle **allusion** to the scar Beloved bears as a result of having her throat cut. Its existence adds another dimension of mystery and suspense to the story.

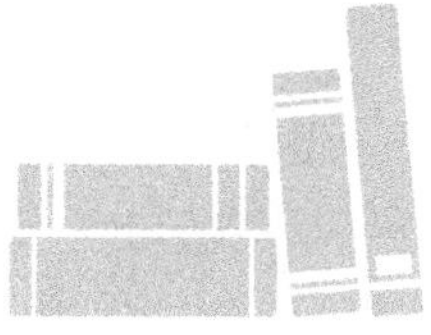

# BELOVED

## TEXTUAL ANALYSIS

## CHAPTER NINE: IT WAS TIME TO LAY IT ALL DOWN

### STRUCTURE

In a series of flashbacks, further **exposition** and characterization are provided. The power of Baby Suggs, holy, her capacity to love, and Sethe's introduction to both Ella and Stamp Paid link the past with the present.

### CHARACTERIZATION

This is an important chapter in terms of characterization for a number of reasons. Baby Suggs, holy, is featured prominently for the first time; Sethe and Denver make decisions that will influence the course of the novel; and the community, in the voices of Ella and Stamp, takes its place among the cast of characters.

More than anyone else Baby Suggs represents many of the novel's important lessons. Through her voice, we learn the importance of self-love and self-possession; that redemption is vital. We are inspired by her capacity to love. Baby Suggs embraces an entire community with words and hope. She opens her home and heart. She is a prime example of the ancestor-elder-rich in wisdom and instruction.

Baby Suggs is also a poignant symbol of defeat. Her response to Sethe's infanticide is chilling because it creates in her a disturbing resignation. Her life, her work, her talk of grace, she believes, is all a lie and she subsequently retires from life in order to ponder "color." Still, she remains a powerful presence in the life of Sethe and Denver. Sethe's trek to the Clearing is testament to that.

Sethe finally appears triumphant. Her walk to the Clearing for solace forces a decision about Paul D; she wants their life. This is a major step in her personal development because it means that she will have to face the memories she has fought so hard to keep down.

Denver's choice-Beloved over Sethe-is another indication of her desire to claim possession of Beloved. While she does manifest concern for her mother over the strangling incident, she is more concerned with keeping her world intact. The picture we get of Denver as a child enhances our understanding of her as she approaches adulthood. A sensitive soul, she is as much a victim as Sethe. Nelson Lord's questions are enough to send Denver reeling, and her reaction-refusing to hear-is a rejection not only of her history but of her mother's as well.

There is also another side of Beloved. Becoming more and more obsessed over Sethe, she shifts from adoring baby-kissing her mother's hurt away-to petulant child, her sense of destructiveness heightened by anything that separates her from Sethe, particularly Paul D. We also get more of a sense of Beloved's otherworldliness; those are her fingers on Sethe's neck.

Two other characters-Ella and Stamp Paid-are voices of the community and will play an important role in the resolution of the novel. Stamp Paid, his name a point of characterization, is highly principled as evidenced by his interaction with the young boy over the coat and the baby. Ella is also principled, and it is significant that her first words of advice to Sethe are "Don't love nothing."

## THEME

Many of the novel's interrelated **themes** and motifs are expressed in this chapter. Here are the lessons of Baby Suggs: the idea of laying it down (redemption); the important lesson of self-love and self-possession, and the underlying tension that exists because white people have so little regard for black life. Beyond these we have the presence or implied presence of Baby Suggs, an ancestral as well as supernatural force and, herself, a symbol of defeat.

Because of Sethe's confusion, Morrison has been able to centralize many of the novel's critical issues. Sethe, in dire need of comfort and advice, seeks the wisdom of the now deceased Baby Suggs. How can she "lay it down" when her memories are so painful? How can she claim ownership-fully claim it-and face the present if she cannot reconcile the past? Sethe's return to the Clearing is important for her emotionally as well as to the novel's thematic structure because she returns to the source, so to speak. She returns to pay homage.

This is the role of the ancestor-elder is Morrison's work, and it becomes important when we look at her attention to the continuum of the black experience.

Just as important is the presence of the supernatural. Sethe feels those fingers on her neck; she feels them choking her; and the fingers, as an omen, add another dimension to the aura of the supernatural that permeates the work.

Baby Suggs, as a symbol of the supernatural in death, represents defeat in life. The nine years she lay in her bed, pondering color as a reaction to Sethe's murderous act, is her way of giving up. "Those white things have taken all I had or dreamed," she says. This is a powerful statement, not only because it articulates one of the major tensions in the novel, but more important because it denies the validity of her life and what she has tried to do with it as a free woman. The family mirrors this defeat as the two boy children, Buglar and Howard, run away from the spite of the house and the women in it.

## METAPHOR

Several instances of **metaphor** exist to signify heightened personal tensions. Baby Suggs' admonishment to "lay it down, sword and shield," puts Sethe's struggle on the level of a personal war. Morrison follows the imagery through with a reference to "her heavy knives of defense."

The images of the cardinal, described as a "blood spot shifting in the trees," and the turtles copulating, turn our attention to the sexual development of Beloved. The search for red becomes a symbol of her own maturation as a woman. The **imagery** of the turtles, however, carries with it a sense of violence and the struggle for dominance.

## SENSE STIMULI

Denver's bout with deafness is another use of the senses to indicate internal conflict. Unable to cope with her mother's past actions or the community's reaction to them, Denver's trauma finds expression in a soundless world.

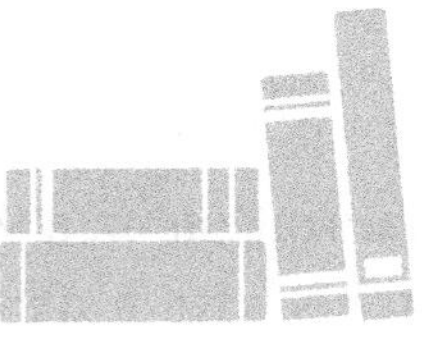

# BELOVED

## TEXTUAL ANALYSIS

## CHAPTER TEN: OUT OF SIGHT ...

### STRUCTURE

Morrison continues the tone she created at the very end of the last chapter in her use of **exposition** regarding Paul D's prison experience in Alfred, Georgia. This is the first chapter in the novel that is all **exposition**. Not only does it signal a momentary lapse in story development as a way to create suspense, but it helps us place the particular incidents in Paul D's life that were, in fact, a turning point in the perception of his own manhood.

### CHARACTERIZATION

The nature of Paul D's character is evinced first by the inner trembling that begins once he is out of Mister's sight; then by his indecisiveness in venturing outside the Indian camp; and finally by his decision to store away the past "in the tobacco tin lodged in his chest." These characteristics further reveal how slavery has affected one black man. Paul D is tentative now, his ability to take control, to make decisions has been thoroughly impaired by his experience at Sweet Home and Alfred, Georgia.

## THEME

One of the most important **themes** to come through in this chapter is that of endurance through the help of the community. In a place so incredibly horrific as Alfred, Georgia, 46 men endure because they learn to trust in their community. This **theme** will be repeated.

## REALISM

Once again, Morrison treats us to realistic details on what slavery and prison life were like for a black man in 19th century America. She also offers particulars on America's treatment of the Cherokees and the historic relationship of cooperation and trust between blacks and Indians during that same period.

## SYMBOLISM

The identification of death and life in male and female terms, respectively, is allegorical. As the men smash the head of Mr. Death and kill the flirt called Life, they create a state of personal limbo for themselves.

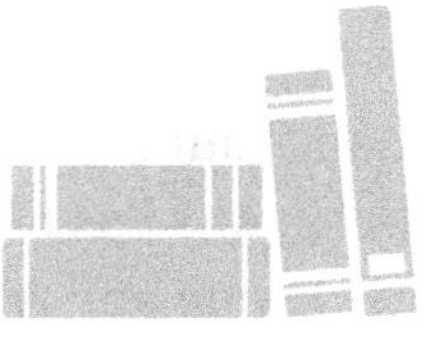

# BELOVED

## TEXTUAL ANALYSIS

## CHAPTER ELEVEN: SHE MOVED HIM

### STRUCTURE

The first sentence mirrors the ambiguity that permeates this chapter. Who is the "she" and what is the movement? Little by little Morrison reveals that she is actually Beloved and that the movement is physical as well as mental; physical in the sense that Paul D moves out of Sethe's bed and finally into the cold room, and mental because ultimately he cannot resist her. Note that Morrison again dates the story; it is now autumn and the nights are growing cold.

### CHARACTERIZATION

Beloved is becoming more and more sophisticated in getting what she wants. The nature of her power is one of the great mysteries of the novel. She is, however, becoming dangerously manipulative.

Paul D gives us another question to ponder. His movement, apparently, is not voluntary. He loves Sethe and wants them to have a life together. Still, he is powerless to resist Beloved, and it is their interaction that opens the "tobacco tin" of his heart. The red heart he didn't have several chapters ago is vibrant and alive-so alive it wakes him up.

## BIBLICAL ALLUSION

One of the biblical references called forth is the story of Lot's wife. Lot and his family, in escaping God's destruction of Sodom (an ancient Palestinian city known for its vice), are warned not to look behind them or they will be "consumed." Lot's wife looks back and as a result is turned into a pillar of salt. A subtle analogy is drawn between Paul D and Lot's wife on the one hand, and Sodom and Beloved on the other: Paul D for his weakness, Beloved for her attractiveness.

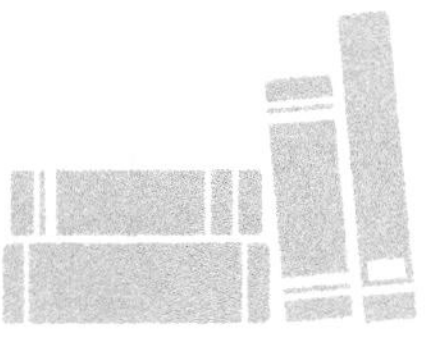

# BELOVED

## TEXTUAL ANALYSIS

## CHAPTER TWELVE: TO GO BACK ...

### CHARACTERIZATION

Denver's obsession with Beloved is the clear focus of this chapter. In particular, we see the effect Beloved has had on Denver-she is more cooperative around the house and certainly more artful in her own manipulation of Beloved. But Denver is also much closer to identifying with her "sister" than she should be. In a kind of surrealistic **episode** that we will see again with Beloved, Denver begins to come apart at the seams when she believes Beloved has left her.

Beloved, for her part, treats it as a game, taunting Denver to come find her-and then disappearing. This is simply one more indication of Beloved's capacity to manipulate others without any regard to their feelings.

Later, as she curls up in a fetal position pointing into the darkness at a face that she sees-Sethe's-she has drawn one more connection. "It's me," she says. There is never any separation of identity for Beloved. Her desire for Sethe, as we shall see later, is a desire to merge.

## SURREALISM

Denver's moment of panic is drawn in surrealistic terms as she feels herself slowly "melting away." Beloved picks up the surrealistic thread as she lies knotted in a fetal position pointing to the face she says is Sethe's and then her own. The use of the surreal here prepares us for the coming chapters when the identities of Denver, Sethe, and Beloved seem to split and merge.

## SENSE IMPRESSION

Once again, the senses are used to telegraph conflict. While Denver may have temporarily lost her hearing as a young child, she gained the enormous power of sight when "she saw every little thing, and colors leaped smoldering into view." Morrison's **imagery** is quite exaggerated-"the most violent of sunsets, stars as fat as dinner plates and all the blood of autumn"-and it illustrates how thoroughly Denver is traumatized by her mother's past.

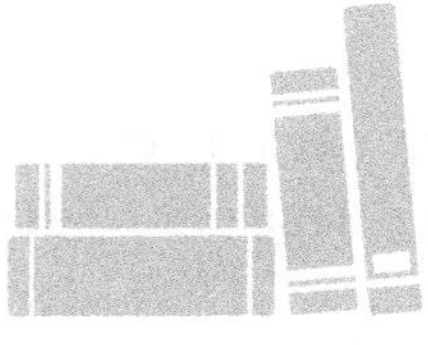

# BELOVED

## TEXTUAL ANALYSIS

## CHAPTER THIRTEEN: THE LAST OF THE SWEET HOME MEN ...

### TIME

It has been three weeks since Paul D found himself settled in the cold house; four months since Beloved's arrival.

### CHARACTERIZATION

Paul D takes center stage as he wrestles not only with a growing sense of powerlessness, but with a key question related to his own identity: What makes a man? Because of his experiences at Sweet Home, the prison in Alfred, Georgia, and now at 124, he questions himself. Stung by his own desire and angered by the feeling that Beloved is manipulating him, he tries to assume control of the situation, i.e., prove his manhood, by asking Sethe to have his baby.

Two sides of Sethe-mother-stoic and lover-come together as Sethe shows first a willingness to accept Paul D and his news no matter how horrible, and second a vulnerability as the two take on the aspect of lovers in their walk home. It is important to note Sethe's claim of Beloved at the end of the chapter. She is finally beginning to feel and know just who Beloved is.

## POINT OF VIEW

Morrison's use of the omniscient voice is masterful in its depiction of a relationship in counterpoint. We hear the interior thoughts of both Sethe and Paul D, and our understanding of their interaction is broadened.

## THEME

Within the context the Sethe and Paul D's relationship is an interesting exploration of male and female. Paul D is a man because he can eat raw meat barely dead; fight raccoons with his hands and win; watch another man roast to death, without shedding a tear. Likewise, the central focus of Sethe's identity is motherhood, which not only encompasses a fierce loyalty and protectiveness as evidenced in her interactions with Paul D over Denver, but "needing to be good enough, alert enough, strong enough, that caring...." These are two different world views, important because of what they say about the quest for personal fulfillment. Paul D's has been an external one. In his wanderings and his freedom he has had to know himself to survive. Sethe's quest has been internal. Given the responsibilities of family, she has had to find herself within that context.

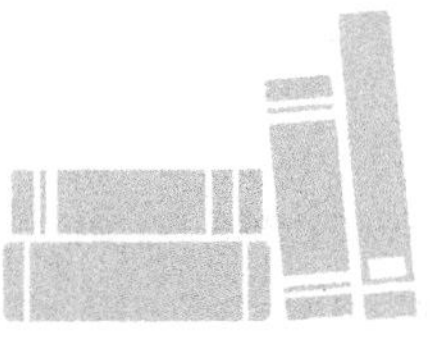

# BELOVED

## TEXTUAL ANALYSIS

## CHAPTER FOURTEEN: DENVER FINISHED WASHING THE DISHES ...

### STRUCTURE

The shortest chapter in the novel, the incident within echoes, in part, the experience Denver had in the barn when she thought Beloved had left her.

### CHARACTERIZATION

Beloved's otherworldliness is magnified by her difficulty in keeping herself physically intact. What better way to show us how tenuous her existence is? She is also more and more petulant; her response to Sethe and Paul D's closeness is an act of self-mutilation. Interesting, too, is the fact that she must be told to cry. Clearly, Beloved is an anomaly.

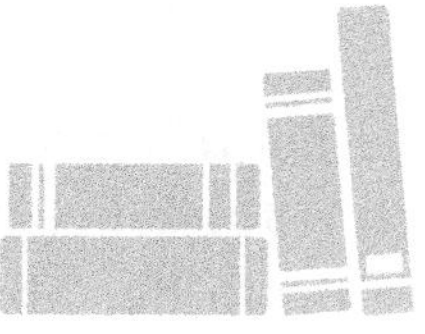

# BELOVED

## TEXTUAL ANALYSIS

## CHAPTER FIFTEEN: IN THE BACK OF BABY SUGGS' MIND ...

### STRUCTURE

Morrison's use of **exposition** to fill in the pieces leading up to Sethe's infanticide heightens the suspense. The **exposition** separates a moment of calm in the story from a major plot development.

### CHARACTERIZATION

Baby Suggs comes further into focus as we gain insight into her impressions and reactions to slavery and freedom. She is a strong and kind woman, and her power, like her sorrow at never knowing her children or herself, is unquestionable. Her role is an important one. Her presence dominates the book because, more than anyone else, she raises the issue of identity, of self-love and self-possession. She also has the kind of wisdom and good-heartedness that symbolizes Morrison's reverence for the ancestor-elder. That is her power and she manifests it in her ability to stretch so little food into so much.

In marked contrast to Sethe, Baby Suggs is stoic and realistic, attitudes that find their home in her perception of motherhood. She is also psychic, relying on her senses as a means of understanding and interpreting the environment.

Additionally, this chapter provides another view of Stamp Paid, who is obviously a kind, sensitive, and generous man, and of the community, which responds as a chorus in their feelings of rage and jealousy at what they perceive to be Baby Suggs' arrogance and excess.

Also introduced in this chapter are Mr. Garner, the owner of Sweet Home; the Bodwins, an abolitionist brother and sister; and Janey Wagon, the Bodwins' young housekeeper.

## THEME

One of the key **themes** in the novel is the effect slavery has on "personhood" and motherhood Baby Suggs is one example, Sethe is another. Yet, it is Baby Suggs who, for Morrison, represents the embodiment of that struggle. She writes, "And no matter, for the sadness was at her center, the desolated center where the self that was no self made its home." This statement reflects the psychological trauma slavery has inflicted upon a people and how they manage to remain people, to define themselves in ways that are meaningful. Out of Baby Suggs' own experience comes the wisdom of the Clearing.

Baby Suggs, who represents the ancestor-elder **theme** as well as the supernatural, is ubiquitous. Her dual presence in the book is witnessed in her interaction with other characters, albeit as a function of memory, and in her spiritual, beyond-the-grave contribution to their lives. This treatment underscores the sense of continuity Morrison establishes between the past and the present. One cannot exist without some integration of the other.

The role of community is also an issue of thematic concern. Baby Suggs' neighbors become angry at her generosity and respond accordingly. They are vengeful in their decision not to warn the household about the posse coming for Sethe and her children. Yet, this is only one side of a complex institution. In later chapters, the community will be as supportive as it once was vengeful.

## REALISM

**Realism** crowds the novel as evidence of slavery's abuses are revealed. Morisson's perspective-the slave perspective-adds a new dimension to historical facts. In this chapter she delves into the familial relations of slaves, their feelings about the marriages they entered, and their need to find family members separated by slavery. A free slave's first magical moments are also described. (Baby Suggs laughs because she can feel her heart beating.)

Also important is the idea and role of religion. The African Methodist Episcopal Church, founded by Bishop Richard Allen, played a tremendous role in the lives of black people. It was the first national organization created by blacks and became a nationwide symbol of power and hope.

## SIMILE AND METAPHOR

Several instances of wordplay must be noted. The first is Morrison's use of **simile**: "berries that tasted like church." The second is her symbolic use of the word "rue": "Carefully with the blade at just the right angle, she [Baby Suggs] cut through a stalk of insistent rue." Rue has two meanings; it is an herb, but it also means sorrow or remorse. Baby Suggs' action becomes an omen. She will not be able to cut through the sorrow she or the community feels as a result of Sethe's act of infanticide.

## BIBLICAL ALLUSION

The three pies that "grew to ten maybe twelve" and the two hens that "became five turkeys" are reminiscent of the Bible story about Jesus taking two fish and five loaves of bread and feeding 5,000 people. This is miracle work, and the image points up the resentment of the community and provides them with reason enough to warn Baby Suggs and Sethe about the approach of Schoolteacher and the slave catcher.

## SENSE STIMULI

The sense of smell for Baby Suggs telegraphs the condemnation of the community and beyond that something "dark and coming." Until now the senses have been used to reflect personal, internal conflict. Their power is extended now to the external. Baby Suggs feels something is wrong because one of her senses tells her so. Interesting is the juxtaposition of the others against olfaction-what she sees and feels purports no danger initially. At the end, however, she is "smelling disapproval, sensing a dark and coming thing and seeing high-topped shoes that she didn't like the look of at all."

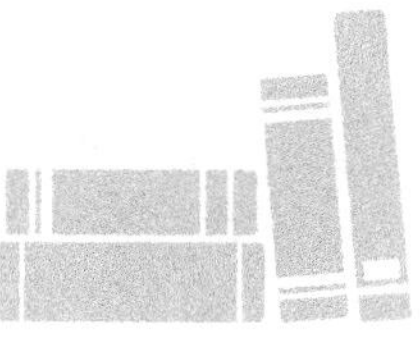

# BELOVED

## TEXTUAL ANALYSIS

## CHAPTER SIXTEEN: WHEN THE FOUR HORSEMEN CAME ...

### STRUCTURE

The **exposition** begun in the previous chapter continues. Morrison finally reveals what happened the day Sethe murdered her daughter. Treated as if it were a secret for more than half the novel, now its pieces fall into place. Morrison, who has provided the factual detail that informed Sethe's decision to commit infanticide, presents the circumstances of the murder. The story can now continue its march forward without digression.

### CHARACTERIZATION

Schoolteacher is a classic example of the use of a tag name. We expect him to be analytical, precise, and matter of fact, and he is. The most revealing aspect of his character, however, is that he sees life as a series of lessons (to be taught). One nephew stays at home to learn his-that you cannot "mishandle creatures and expect success."

We also feel a certain hardheartedness about him. His reaction to Sethe's act of murder is in marked contrast to his nephew's who, stunned and shaken, can only ask, "What she want to go and do that for?" It is no time before Schoolteacher, having made his assessment, is out the door, his superiority intact.

Another point of characterization comes in the reaction of the community to the happenings at 124. They are less than supportive in their reaction to Sethe's deed; they are quite small, in fact. In a situation this tragic, they search for arrogance in Sethe and refuse to embrace her in song as she leaves the house with her baby in her arms.

Sethe is traumatized by her act, but her instinct to nurture transcends all. This is key to understanding her character, for motherhood means everything to Sethe.

Baby Suggs' reaction is also telling. Far from judgmental, she acts out of concern for the children who remain, all the while asking God's forgiveness. Her faith is so severely shaken that ultimately the only recourse left is to retire to bed and ponder color.

## POINT OF VIEW

The use of another voice to introduce the chapter captures the sense of urgency and desperation that a slave on the run must have felt. The voice, however, is the slave catcher's. The text then shifts into an **exposition** that reflects the view not of our principal characters, but of Schoolteacher, the one nephew and the sheriff. Note the use of the word "nigger," as well as the tone of the text. Morrison captures the sense of superiority, but also the indifference to human life that slavery bred into some men.

## METAPHOR

The comparison of the slave to an animal, present here in the description of Stamp and the sounds he makes-"grunting" and "mewing"-and in Schoolteacher's analogy of the hounds, continues and is echoed in his reflection that blacks need care and guidance to civilize them and "keep them from the cannibal life they preferred." This was an important justification for many for the existence and perpetuation of slavery.

## SYMBOLISM

The high-topped shoes Baby Suggs saw in the previous chapter become a symbol, a reminder, even in the midst of tragedy, of her place in society.

## IRONY

A major **irony** feeds the novel in its exploration of slavery and its impact on people. In this chapter it becomes real. Sethe tries to murder the one thing she professes to love more than anything in the world-her children-and succeeds in killing one.

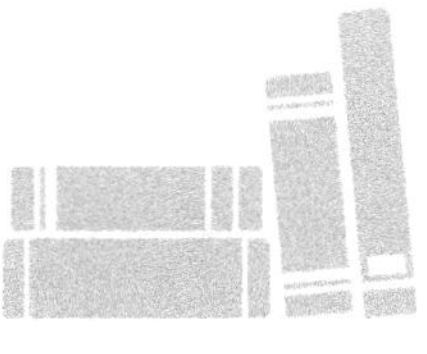

# BELOVED

## TEXTUAL ANALYSIS

## CHAPTER SEVENTEEN: THAT AIN'T HER MOUTH

### STRUCTURE

The opening sentence is the modulating force in the progression of the chapter. It is a denial set against the affirmation of a newspaper clipping and Stamp's own recollection of his role in the events that led up to the death of the infant. Morrison is able to heighten the suspense, because Paul D cannot read, and Stamp must muster the courage and the words to tell the story. Bit by bit, the pieces fall into place. But Paul D is busy in his denial, and cannot accept even the words in a newspaper article.

### CHARACTERIZATION

Paul D's denial is a function of how much he has grown to care for Sethe. We already know, however, that they have different attitudes about loving-hers is all-consuming, his is moderated by circumstance-and we can surmise what his ultimate reaction will be.

Stamp Paid, as the purveyor of bad news, feels he is doing what he has to do. Once again, we see his principles in action.

The community, as seen through Stamp's eyes, also functions as a character. He attributes a meanness to them, suggests an envy that gives the community a life of its own.

## REALISM

The details surrounding the role of Cincinnati in the slaughterhouse industry, the growth of the city, and the flow of progress provide a realistic setting for the events that take place in this chapter. Morrison, in her use of the newspaper clipping, also points to the sensationalistic treatment of blacks by the media.

## THEME

The supernatural is present in Morrison's brief description of the cemetery and its disturbed residents. Even Paul D is not immune to the voices that he hears; it is a kind of haunting. Stamp's recollection of Baby Suggs' heightened sensibilities, as evidenced in the previous chapter, reinforces that. Both are taken as a matter of course.

Also at issue is Stamp's role as ancestor-elder. He assumes the responsibility of telling Paul D of Sethe's past. Although we may question his wisdom or motivation for doing so, he is acting out of a desire to inform and protect, both important functions of the ancestor-elder.

## SIMILE

The extended **simile** used to describe Sethe's sense of urgency and flight at Schoolteacher's arrival is revealing. Stamp recalls she acted like a "hawk on the wing," "her face beaked," and her "hands working like claws." Sethe will pick up this image in the next chapter when she admits "she heard wings."

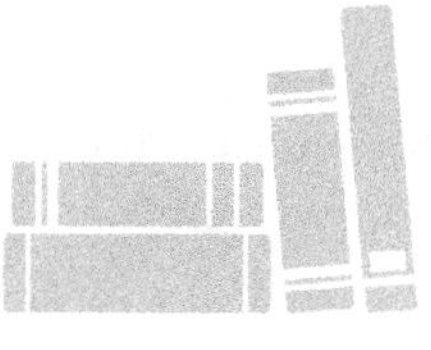

# BELOVED

## TEXTUAL ANALYSIS

## CHAPTER EIGHTEEN: "SHE WAS CRAWLING ALREADY ..."

### STRUCTURE

Finally, Sethe has an opportunity to tell her side of the story. It is a turning point in the novel because how and what she articulates will determine whether she returns to the isolating life she had before Paul D or go on with him to a new life. Morrison balances Sethe's slow and meandering confession with Paul D's gradual reaction. It becomes an epiphany for him as he realizes the depths of Sethe's love. He is also called on to make a judgment, just as we must. Was Sethe right or wrong in killing her child?

### CHARACTERIZATION

Our understanding of Sethe's nurturing instinct (maternal love), her feelings and dedication to it, is deepened as she tries to explain what that instinct drove her to do. In her confession, she digresses in order to make us understand that she gave all she had and wanted to give more; that her escape from slavery, while instilling in her a sense of confidence and knowledge of her own power, also freed her to love more fully; and that that love was so profound and so protective it could only manifest in the way that it did.

Paul D's response, as well as his decision to leave, is an echo of the community's in part because of his guilt-shame over Beloved, but also in fear that Sethe's "love is too thick" and out of righteousness that "what she did was wrong." Thus, our sense of Paul D is enlarged beyond the portrait of a man wrestling with his own sense of powerlessness to that of a man wrestling with the sense of power one woman claims to possess.

## CONFLICT

What Sethe articulates as mother love is, according to the dictates of society, unacceptable and represents a distortion. Yet, Sethe's act, however unforgivable, is not an act in isolation of experience. Sethe was a slave. She knows firsthand the horrors of that. She also knows freedom and the sense of self-possession that comes with it. This is one of the principal conflicts in the novel and raises several questions about who we are and how we love.

## THEME

The exploration of mother love, especially under the effects of slavery, is a key **theme** in this chapter. Sethe's desire to protect her children, while understandable, has dire consequences.

There is also the male-female aspect. Paul D and Sethe each define themselves according to their own experiences. Slavery as a particular aspect of that experience has created within them two different ways of looking at the world: Sethe's quest for identity stopped at motherhood; Paul D's search took him outside himself. His statement, "This here new Sethe didn't know where the world stopped and she began," is important. It marks a basic distinction between the two.

## SIMILE

Sethe's act of moving around the room is compared to a spinning wheel and becomes a physical manifestation of what she is doing mentally in trying to recount the story. There is no way to tell it straight, so she moves around it, circling it, never honing in on the act itself.

## SYMBOLISM

There are a number of symbols to communicate the varying tension created in Sethe and Paul D as a result of her past. The milk, which has been used over and over again as a symbol of motherhood, takes on even greater proportions as Sethe explains, "the milk was all I ever had."

The hummingbirds, certainly a symbol of flight for Sethe, also signify an urgency. The hummingbird, noted for its long beak and ability to fly backward or forward, has one of the fastest wing beasts of any bird in existence.

The two remaining symbols-the forest and the number of Sethe's feet are related to each other in that they become images of separation. Paul D's reminder to Sethe that she has two feet, not four, i.e., that she is not an animal, crafts a forest between them. More than just distance, however, the forest implies a blindness. As a man, Paul D has neither the same experience nor vision that Sethe has as slave, mother, and free woman.

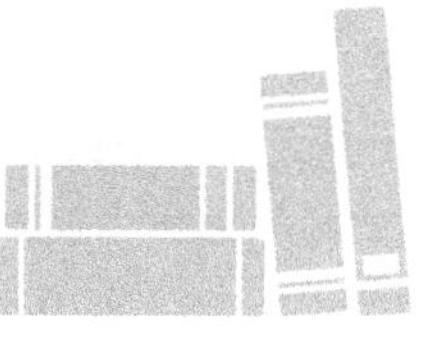

# BELOVED

## TEXTUAL ANALYSIS

## CHAPTER NINETEEN: 124 WAS LOUD

### STRUCTURE

Immediately, we know that something is amiss. Where before 124 was spiteful-an internal conflict existing between its residents living and dead it is now "loud." Morrison expands on the notion of haunting, while enlarging our sense of the cultural milieu in which Sethe lives. Similarly, she continues to use memory and personal reflection as a means of furthering **exposition** and characterization. Additionally, Morrison dates the movement of the novel. It is now winter, 1874.

### CHARACTERIZATION

We are learning more and more about Stamp Paid, Sethe, Baby Suggs, and Ella, who functions in many respects as the voice of the community. The complexity of their interaction with each other, or lack thereof, gives us insight into their characters.

With regard to Stamp Paid, we finally learn how he got his name, and as a consequence that he is a very principled man. His ties to Baby Suggs extend beyond the grave and as leader-elder, he has a moderating influence on the conscience of the community.

He is a deeply caring and committed man, a believer in "truth and forewarning," and in an interesting turnabout on the word sneak, he is a sneak, albeit for a good cause. These virtues prompt him to face Sethe and the guilt he carries because of his decision to tell Paul D her secret.

The character of Sethe as victim-stoic takes on a greater sense of urgency. With Paul D gone, she finally realizes Beloved is her daughter returned from the grave. It is the beginning of what will be a slow and steady decline. Troubled for many years over recriminations, she is alternately guilt-ridden, resigned, angry, and proud.

Her need to make things right fuels endless monologues that attempt to justify her decision to commit infanticide. Just as important, she further isolates herself from the community in exchange for a life inside 124; there is no world beyond her door.

Ella's role, like Stamp's, is a function of the community. She, too, is highly principled, but in her we see an unforgivingness, a tendency toward harsh judgments. Later, she will soften.

Baby Suggs comes to light through the eyes of Stamp. "The mountain to his sky," she is a strong woman defeated finally by the losses in her life, but most especially by Sethe's murder of her grandchild, which is triggered by "whitefolks" coming into her yard. Her response is telling, too. She opts for a self-imposed isolation in retiring to her bed to ponder color.

We are also given further insight into the character of Schoolteacher, understanding more and more why he is so named. Convinced of his own superiority, he treats the slaves as if they were experiments: poking prodding, and analyzing them for their animal and human characteristics.

## THEME

**Themes** and motifs in this chapter include the presence of the supernatural; a ringing indictment of slavery, racism, and the system or community of people who practiced and justified such violence against others; memory as catharsis; isolation, defeat, possession, redemption, stoicism, and ancestry.

We are already familiar with Morrison's position on the supernatural; it is an accepted part of life. The voices that Stamp says ring the house at 124 are, he believes, voices from the past, the ancestors. Morrison also writes they are the voices of Sethe, Denver, and Beloved. Thus, the natural and the supernatural co-exist, feeding and supporting one another.

The indictment of slavery and racism come through as never before as the characters themselves examine their experiences with "whitefolks." Stamp Paid wants to know "What are these people?" Baby Suggs literally gives up because "they came in my yard." Halle believes they are all alike, and Sethe refuses "any more news about whitefolks ... about the world done up the way whitefolks loved it."

Within this framework comes the use of memory as catharsis. Every recollection takes on an added importance because it is a working through of the past. Sethe's willingness to remember is a function of her need to be forgiven, to be purged of the years of guilt and remorse over Baby Suggs and Beloved.

The issues of isolation, defeat, possession, redemption, and stoicism give depth to the portrayal of Sethe as a woman in trouble. It is her stoicism and defeat that bring about the reaction of isolation and the need for redemption. And it is the sense of possession-as evidenced by the word "mine," the only word decipherable among the voices ringing the house-that feeds the cycle. Possession in this case, however, is not about the self, as Baby Suggs taught, but about others. Denver and Sethe both claim Beloved while Beloved only has eyes for Sethe. This idea comes up again and again and forms the basis of the novel's conclusion.

Certain incidents pick up on these threads, but it's particularly evident in the kind of self-imposed isolation Sethe and the girls adopt. They ice skate and no one sees them falling; Stamp Paid knocks and no one answers; Sethe does not notice the tracks in the snow. The three exist in a world all their own, seemingly harmless at first, but fraught with danger. Even Morrison's description of Baby Suggs' funeral years earlier carries the same seeds; Denver and Sethe are on one side, the community is on the other.

## REALISM

There are several interjections of historical detail that add to our understanding of and provide the context for what life was like for a slave once free. This is 1874-11 years after the Emancipation

Proclamation and 9 years after the end of the Civil War. Through Sethe's memories, Morrison points to the important issues and events of the abolitionist era: manumission and the Dred Scott decision; black abolitionist Frederick Douglass' North Star newspaper; and the atmosphere of hostility that existed toward blacks as well as the personal, internal conflicts it spawned in both races.

## SYMBOLISM

Stamp's red ribbon, attached to part of a scalp he pulls from the water, takes on a dual meaning-as a reminder of slavery's horrors and a testament to black people's endurance.

## WORDPLAY

The use of both **simile** and **metaphor** is everywhere in this chapter. The power and magic of Morrison's language comes alive in vibrant images. Note the following examples in **similes** like:

"... his belated concern, scorching his soul like a silver dollar in a fool's pocket."

"Their skirts flew like wings and their skin turned pewter in the cold and dying light."

Or the following **metaphor** representing Sethe's joy at regaining the lost treasure of Beloved:

"A hobnail casket of jewels found in a tree hollow should be fondled before it is opened. Its lock may have rusted or broken away from the clasp. Still you should touch the nail heads, and test its weight. No smashing with an ax head before it is decently exhumed from the grave that has hidden it all this time."

Furthermore, Sethe's ascension of the "lily-white stairs like a bride" comes to symbolize the beginning of a new life and the love she hopes to share with her two girls. The image is extended several pages later with Sethe's desire to "fondle the day and circumstances of Beloved's arrival and the meaning of that kiss in the Clearing."

## IRONY

Sethe's belief that she doesn't have to explain and her persistent need to is an example of dramatic irony.

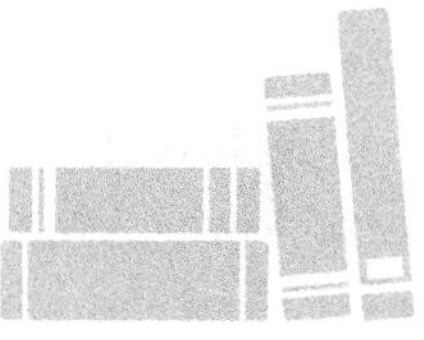

# BELOVED

## TEXTUAL ANALYSIS

## CHAPTER TWENTY: BELOVED, SHE MY DAUGHTER

### STRUCTURE

This is the first in a series of chapters that use the stream-of-consciousness technique to establish the psychological state of a particular character. Here, it is Sethe. A long series of rambling thoughts turns into a monologue directed at Beloved in another attempt to justify her decision to commit infanticide.

### CHARACTERIZATION

Sethe explores fully the issue of motherhood from her perspective as a child born to a slave mother and as a freed slave woman trying to keep her children from experiencing the same horror. The first two sentences are important clues to her state of mind because they establish the issue of possession. Beloved belongs to her. Later she proffers the idea that she belongs to Beloved. This is the beginning of an obsessive relationship. Sethe's need to explain, to make Beloved understand, is gigantic and becomes her reason for living.

The second point is made with a symbol we have seen before-the milk. Sethe draws a strong connection between milk and motherhood, mother's milk being the source of a baby's nourishment and therefore its life.

She also talks about her relationship with her own mother in a childish, even whimsical way. Obviously this is something Sethe yearned for, missed, in fact, and remains fanciful about. This connection, or lack of, informs Sethe's own attitudes about motherhood. She tries to compensate for the absence of her mother by being what she thinks is the perfect mother. Morrison writes:

"You [Beloved] came right on back like a good girl, like a daughter which is what I wanted to be and would have been if my ma'am had been able to get out of the rice long enough before they hanged her and let me be one."

For Sethe, however, being perfect also means surviving, and she continues to live because she has other children to think about.

In what comes to be a magnificent evocation of Sethe's inner world, we see again the many nuances that drove her to murder. The experience of slavery has so distorted her concept of self and motherhood, she has no recourse. Having tasted freedom, a return to slavery for her, and most especially for her children, is a fate worse than death.

## THEME

This chapter explores a number of interrelated themes-motherhood, identity, possession. Sethe's perception of motherhood includes possession and more. It is sacrifice and survival; nourishment and instruction. It also becomes a reflection of intergenerational conflicts; a sense of continuity exists beginning with Sethe's mother through Sethe and on to Beloved and Denver. This is at the heart of Sethe's struggle for identity. In order for her to go on, to fully claim possession of herself, she will have to resolve these conflicts and accept the limitations of motherhood.

## POINT OF VIEW

In a major shift, Morrison steps back as omniscient narrator and allows us to hear Sethe's voice alone. In doing so, Morrison affords us insight into Sethe's temperament. Her explanations reveal a lot about her. More and more we gain insight into the many forces that have affected her behavior.

## SYMBOLISM

The milk, because of its nutritional properties, represents motherhood. It is a symbol we have seen before.

## SENSE STIMULI

Two reactions are important for what they tell us about character. We are aware of Baby Suggs' decision to ponder color, to live her life through the sense of sight. This thread is picked up by Sethe as she points out that the pink in Beloved's headstone was the last color she saw until the point at which she recognized the young woman as her own. Also, Sethe's bout with stuttering, after the death of her mother, is an indication of ongoing inner conflicts.

# BELOVED

## TEXTUAL ANALYSIS

## CHAPTER TWENTY-ONE: BELOVED IS MY SISTER

### STRUCTURE

This is the second of four chapters that interrupt the command of the omniscient narrator in order to furnish insight into a particular character. Using once again the stream-of-consciousness technique. Morrison exposes the trauma and subsequent vulnerability that are Denver's.

### CHARACTERIZATION

Denver is the troubled daughter of a troubled mother. Traumatized by Sethe's one act of violence, she has grown up in a self-imposed isolation-removing herself physically from the world, even refusing to hear at one time. In her loneliness, she cultivates a relationship with the baby ghost and now with Beloved. Her sense of protectiveness is strong. So is her need to love and be loved.

Denver's voice is not that of an adult, however. We hear the fanciful imagination of a child as she talks about her father as an "angel man"; the terror of having her hair braided every night; and her almost mystical regard for Baby Suggs. More important, we learn that Denver's response to her mother and the world comes out of Sethe's one murderous act, thus fear immobilizes her and waiting for her daddy is the only thing that gives her hope.

## THEME

The need to possess is a **theme** explored in the triangular relationship of Sethe, Denver, and Beloved in this chapter. Denver articulates it very well. At the same time, she gives us insight into the nature of her own mother-daughter conflict. Also echoed in this chapter are Baby Suggs' lesson of self-love and Denver's supernatural gift (her early memories are uncanny).

## POINT OF VIEW

The use of the first person moves us inside the head of Denver. This is important now so that we can understand the various dynamics operating in the relationships among the three women. So far, we have heard Sethe, driven by a need to explain and make things right, and Denver, who is just as possessive in her need to love and be loved, but how is also the moderating force between Beloved and Sethe.

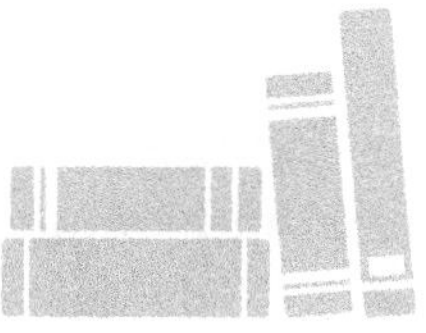

# BELOVED

## TEXTUAL ANALYSIS

## CHAPTER TWENTY-TWO: I AM BELOVED AND SHE IS MINE. I SEE ...

### STYLE

In what is the most surrealistic event in the novel, Beloved speaks, not just for herself, but as a representative of the 60 million Africans taken from their homeland who died in the middle passage. To mark its importance, Morrison suspends formal grammatical requirements, opting instead for short staccato-like sentences with very little punctuation of capitalization. As in the previous two chapters, the style of the prose is stream-of-consciousness. We are finally inside Beloved's head.

### CHARACTERIZATION

Clearly, Beloved is something other than Sethe's daughter returned from the dead. Her memory spans beyond the immediate past to Africa and the middle passage and collects the experiences of the men and women who were stolen from their homeland and never seen again.

Beyond that, Beloved struggles to identify and merge with Sethe. In the place beyond, she searches for her face and, in fact, wants to be that face. There can be no separation, just possession. This desire is very strong in Beloved and, as we shall see later, almost comes to pass.

One interesting point of characterization with regard to Sethe is Beloved's insistence that her mother whispered to her, calling her back.

## SURREALISM

Reality turns surrealistic in Beloved's hands. Her thoughts are disjointed, measured out in short staccato bursts, and her memory has a timeless quality. This makes the chapter very different from the rest of the book because it calls attention to a very important quality of Beloved's-her otherworldliness.

## THEME

The supernatural finds its place not only in Beloved as its central representative, but in the powerful presence of the Africans who never made it to these shores. Morrison, while not giving them a voice per se, articulates their experience and thus interweaves another aspect of slavery - the response of black people toward their own captivity. Other **themes** have to do with Beloved's equation of identity with possession: her desire to merge is tangible; it is a "hot thing."

## METAPHOR

Beloved's use of the words "a hot thing" becomes a **metaphor** for desire. She wants the face, the smile, and finally the merge. These are all "hot things." Additionally, chewing and swallowing take on larger than life proportions. More than just representing the physical act of consumption, the two actions signify a kind of devouring. So strong is Beloved's desire to merge with Sethe that she wants to engulf and be engulfed by the older woman. This **imagery** will be used again and again.

Another interesting use of symbolism is Beloved's connection to water. Introduced first as a symbol of life in an earlier chapter, it takes on the added meaning of death, e.g., the dead and dying are thrown into the sea and those who wish to die refuse water; and later it is a symbol of rebirth when Beloved steps out of the water alive.

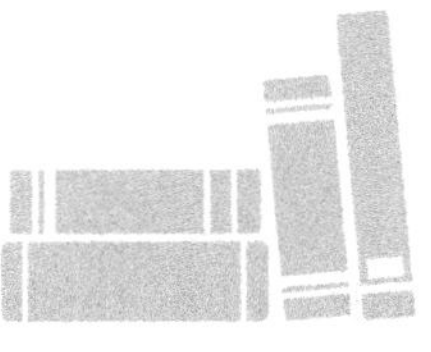

# BELOVED

## TEXTUAL ANALYSIS

## CHAPTER TWENTY-THREE: I AM BELOVED AND SHE IS MINE. SETHE IS ...

### STYLE

This chapter, as an extension of the previous three, begins in the stream-of-consciousness thought of Beloved. In direct contrast to the preceding chapter, however, there are no more staccato sentences and the rules of punctuation and capitalization are followed precisely. This chapter also picks up the middle-passage imagery.

Following the page break, the chapter moves into a kind of free-verse dialogue. Sethe and Beloved talk. Denver and Beloved talk. All three talk. Yet, the tone is still surrealistic. There are moments of connection and digression created to focus attention once again on the changing dynamics of Denver, Sethe, and Beloved's relationship.

## SURREALISM

To emphasize the different perspectives of Sethe, Beloved, and Denver, Morrison uses a surrealistic approach. The voices often seem to be operating exclusive of the conversation that was meant. For example, Denver remembers that she and Beloved played together. Beloved knows only that she needs Sethe. Later, Morrison returns to her use of short, staccato sentences and a lack of punctuation to focus on those divergences.

## THEME

For Beloved, identity and possession come through as consuming passions. For Denver and Sethe possession is enough. Note the repetition of possessives: "I want her face," "You are mine," "I have your milk." In their desire to possess one or the other, each has become more and more obsessed.

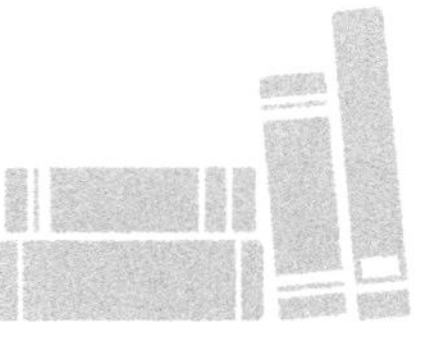

# BELOVED

## TEXTUAL ANALYSIS

## CHAPTER TWENTY-FOUR: IT WAS A TINY CHURCH NO BIGGER THAN A RICH MAN'S PARLOR

### STRUCTURE

Paul D becomes the vehicle for further **exposition**. This suspension in story line, a technique Morrison uses repeatedly, creates tension around what's happening at 124. The **exposition**, however, provides more background on the atmosphere at Sweet Home prior to the escape, as well as the sense of family that existed among the slaves there.

### CHARACTERIZATION

Paul D struggles with his doubts, his feeling of powerlessness, and his sense of manhood. He is still trying to come to terms with the experience of slavery and how it has affected his life. He has no family to speak of (his one attempt with Sethe having failed) and he is beginning to question why it all went wrong. He is not alone in his query, though. We know Sethe has wondered the same thing, too.

Within the context of Paul D's experience and his interpretation of life's events, Sixo becomes a character of contrast. In this chapter, he comes alive for us. Sixo is a real man in Paul D's eyes because he fights back, he values his own sense of manhood and does not back down. His death is a testament to that.

Schoolteacher and Garner also become characters of comparison: the former noted for his tyrannical and inhuman treatment of the slaves, the latter for his relative humanity.

## THEME

Defeat has hit all of the major characters in their attempts to build a life outside of slavery. Baby Suggs is defeated by Sethe's actions and the men who came into her yard. Sethe faces defeat when Schoolteacher seeks her out, and she is later defeated by her memories. Paul D is defeated by Beloved in their competition for Sethe's affections and by the revelation of Sethe's infanticide. Defeat becomes a motif that Morrison uses to round out her characterizations and to support the **theme** of slavery's impact on the slaves.

## REALISM

As an institution, slavery tended to destroy the concept of family, as Morrison points out, but there were instances where slave families did survive and come together. The institution of family and extended family within the slave community was an important one. Marriages, although not legally recognized, were celebrated with ceremony, and many slaves lived in marriages of 30 years or more. Men and women were also expected to stay faithful within the marriage and fathers were strong and respected members of the community.

This chapter also provides further background on the atrocities of slavery and the arrogance and assumed superiority of many slave owners.

## METAPHOR

Sixo's hatred is described as "so loose, it was juba." Juba is a southern dance of black origin that is accompanied by rhythmic hand clapping and slapping of the thighs.

## IRONY

We have already pointed out the **irony** in Morrison's naming of the plantation Sweet Home. Such **irony** is extended as a result of the treatment the slaves received. Called a "craddle" and "a wonderful lie," life at Sweet Home was not at all representative of the average slave experience-that is, until Schoolteacher arrived.

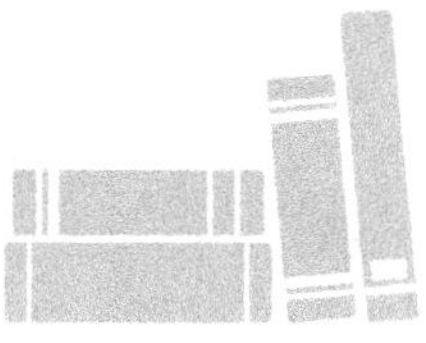

# BELOVED

## TEXTUAL ANALYSIS

## CHAPTER TWENTY-FIVE: "HOWDY"

### CHARACTERIZATION

The interaction between Paul D and Stamp reinforces our sense of who these characters are. Like Sethe, Paul D refuses to make plans, and he finds temporary solace in a bottle while struggling to put the pieces of his life together. Obviously tired, he asks what is, for many, a very important question-"How much is a nigger supposed to take?" Stamp's response is (like Stamp) very basic and very stoic. Stamp's is the voice of reason and also of the elder. Steady in his wisdom and sense of caring, he represents the best elements of community and is far less judgmental when it comes to Sethe. His decision to remain silent about the whereabouts of Judy attests to that commitment to community. Also important, Stamp recounts in detail how he got his name. As a tag name, Stamp Paid is a principal means of characterization. His early sacrifice of wife and relationship, he feels, has rendered him debtless.

## REALISM

Morrison adds more historical detail as she examines briefly the relationship between the races. The white man on his Eastern saddle assumes a superior and patriarchal tone in his concern that Paul D not drink on the church steps. Stamp's response is quick and knowing; he defers and thus eradicates a potentially volatile situation.

## SYMBOLISM

Stamp's red ribbon comes to us again as a dual symbol of slavery's horrors and black people's ability to endure. His constant manipulation of it seems to suggest that this is where he gets some of his strength.

## IRONY

Paul D's initial response to Stamp Paid is noticeably sarcastic: "If it's hard for you, might kill me dead."

He is justifiably angry and skeptical. Stamp has caused a major upheaval in his life.

# BELOVED

## TEXTUAL ANALYSIS

## CHAPTER TWENTY-SIX: 124 WAS QUIET

### STRUCTURE

From spiteful to loud to quiet, the personification of 124 continues as a way to illustrate the tenor of relationships within the house. Further **exposition** informs us that the silence is a measure of the open power struggle between Sethe and Beloved. The chapter ends ambiguously, however, with the resolution of that struggle intimated but not defined. As she has done throughout the novel, Morrison dates movement in the story line. In this chapter we go from January through at least June.

### CHARACTERIZATION

Certain aspects of each character's personality are tempered by present circumstance. Denver develops compassion for her mother and moves out beyond the world of 124 to save them both. Sethe's guilt and remorse literally overtake her and she is diminished. Beloved's constant need for love and attention turns destructive as she saps the lifeblood from Sethe. Ella, highly judgmental and standing back from Sethe's predicament, becomes avenger, as do many of the community's women. This response to crisis is a major point of characterization.

Denver's growth is most astonishing. In her late teens but more child than woman, she is forced to look beyond herself and her loneliness to come to terms with her mother and move on. As she seeks help first from Lady Jones then the Bodwins, her world grows larger and with it her ability to cope. Denver claims herself. It is an important lesson. Self-love and self-possession, important **themes** in the novel, come to her as a result.

Sethe, on the other hand, becomes a tragic symbol of defeat. Her one real flaw-loving her children too much, believing that they are, indeed, her "best thing"-damages her as much if not more than the years of repressed guilt and remorse over Beloved's murder. Having lost her job and all contact with the outside world, she ironically negates her responsibility as mother to Denver and spends her time trying to right a wrong that cannot be corrected. Her decline is regrettable and in direct contrast to Denver's personal and Beloved's physical growth.

Our portrait of Sethe grows even more complex because we are privy to the psychological turmoil that has existed within her for so many years. Beloved's presence as ghost and "human-other" has, by turns, assuaged and intensified that turmoil. We cannot question her existence. We see her, others see her, but we must accept that Sethe's preoccupation over the murder and her subsequent guilt fuel an unwillingness to let go of the past. Sethe is responsible for bringing Beloved into the physical realm once Paul D has exorcised the baby ghost. She needs the reminder because her sense of self is so locked into her children and memorialized in Beloved's death and resurrection.

Beloved feeds on Sethe's madness, too. Her need to be loved, her indifference to explaining her actions make Sethe try that much harder to justify those actions. There can be no justification, however. Beloved's need is all-consuming and her food is a willing Sethe; she swallows her "mother" whole.

The chapter also extends the sense of otherworldliness in Beloved. The surrealistic memories of gazing at a face in the water, picking flowers, and massaging the "pretty white points" of the face in front of her take on real life proportions as Beloved enacts them all.

Ella, as rescuer, shows us another side of a woman whose harsh judgments seemed to signal an unyielding quality about her. Practical and unsentimental, she turns Sethe's rescue into a religious crusade. Her ability to harness the energy of the community's women in order to save Sethe makes her a woman of strength and compassion.

Each of the other characters-Lady Jones, Mr. Bodwin, and Janey-adds in his or her own way to the nature of community. Lady Jones is an educated, "yellow" black woman who has spent her life teaching the community's children. Mr. Bodwin is the benevolent white man abolitionist, who, fighting age and boredom, finds peace in the simple pleasures of life. Janey Wagon, as another voice of the community, is alternately concerned, curious, and high-minded about Sethe's state of affairs. These characters are not drawn as fully as Sethe or Paul

D or Denver. They do not have to be, because they represent the best and worst of what the community can be.

## THEME

Sethe's isolation, while putting the entire family at risk, becomes even more dangerous as she surrenders to Beloved. Within this context, subsequent events support many of the **themes** and motifs of the work, i.e., self-love and self-possession; the role of the ancestor-elder; the presence of the supernatural; the role of the community; redemption; isolation; and the mother-daughter conflict.

Central to the development of these issues is Denver, whose actions are the impetus for the chapter's **climax**. Finally realizing the precarious nature of Sethe and Beloved's relationship, she is forced to take possession of herself and to accept her mother's past. This resolution of the mother-daughter conflict is what allows Denver to move on. Beloved, on the other hand, keeps Sethe trapped.

Additionally, we see the positive contributions of the ancestor-elder. At the point of Denver's greatest doubts, Baby Suggs offers instruction and encouragement from beyond the grave. Her voice is the voice of the supernatural. Her spiritual presence in the work is as powerful as her physical presence once was.

What is even more telling is the community's response to Beloved's intrusion. With an almost unabashed acceptance of Beloved as Sethe's daughter returned from the dead, the women show us how deep their belief in the supernatural lies.

Thus, the community becomes rescuer. Once distant and judgmental, they reach out to Sethe at her darkest hour. Their warmth and concern help to pull her back, and that action focuses our attention on the dual nature of community. As vital as the people who compose it, it responds as though it were human itself: judgmental on the one hand, nurturing on the other.

The end result for Sethe is a kind of redemption. Will she, as Baby Suggs so often instructed, be able to "lay it all down"? This has been the question all along, for coming to terms with the past has meant having a life.

## REALISM

Another realistic aspect of Morrison's narrative comes out of her characterization of Lady Jones. Color-consciousness was a fact of life in the black community. Many mulattoes lived with the stigma of being "high yellow." Envied and often rejected by the black community, they found no solace in the white one. In many instances, however, the lighter a black person was, the better his or her opportunities might be. Many extremely light-skinned black people "passed" for white.

## SYMBOLISM

Beloved's scar, described as "a smile in the kootchy-kootchy-coo place under her chin," is, ironically, not something ugly, but something pleasing, and represents Sethe's inability to be reconciled with her actions of 18 years ago. Beyond the scar is the larger symbol of Beloved herself. Not only is she a measure of Sethe's guilt but the vehicle for her redemption. Furthermore, Ella extends the religious motif by making Beloved's banishment a struggle between good and evil.

Other symbols-the image of Beloved as Medusa (mythical Greek character), "with vines of hair twisted all over her head," and the hummingbirds, a recurring symbol of urgency and flight for Sethe-bring to the action a heightened sense of conflict. Medusa's danger lay in her ability to captivate and destroy, turning the beholder into stone with one glance. She represents Beloved's goal, although not a goal achieved through Beloved's methods. The hummingbirds are like alarms that go off in Sethe's head. "No, no no," is what they tell her.

## HUMOR

Morrison's description of Denver's dress, "so loud it embarrassed the needlepoint chair seat," as well as her sense of **irony** (see discussion below), provides a well-timed comic relief. The chapter's tension, steadily building toward a **climax**, is eased momentarily by this display of humor.

## IRONY

There are several ironies at work here; they are both humorous and dramatic. Morrison's use of language pinpoints two immediately: Baby Suggs' "this ain't a battle; it's a rout" and Ella's "She didn't mind a little communication between the two worlds, but this was an invasion" are fine examples of ironic humor.

The instances of dramatic **irony** include Denver's perception that she must now protect her mother from Beloved when for so long it was the other way around. Sethe's inability to see that Beloved is pregnant, that Beloved is becoming the Sethe of 20 years ago, is another. The existence of a demeaning slave figurine in the kitchen of an abolitionist's house is still another.

## METAPHOR/SIMILE

Morrison's use of both **simile** and **metaphor** is very strong. To heighten the tension, she uses images that are rife with a sense of foreboding. For example:

"By the end of March the three of them looked like carnival women with nothing to do."

"She [Beloved] was not like them. She was wild game."

"Then Sethe spit up something she had not eaten and it rocked Denver like a gunshot."

## BIBLICAL ALLUSION

Ella's biblical reference, "Sufficient unto the day is the evil thereof," is taken from Matthew 6. In a chapter that expounds on human behavior, the apostle advocates steadiness, humility, and a close adherence to God's word as important keys to survival. In essence, we must take life one day at a time.

## SENSE STIMULI

Throughout the novel, the senses are not only a medium by which we interpret the world, but a way to reflect the unresolved conflicts in individuals. When Denver meets Nelson Lord again and he speaks, she feels herself, and in particular her hearing, open up like a flower. Sethe, too, responds to the "sound" the women make, trembling "like the baptized in its wash."

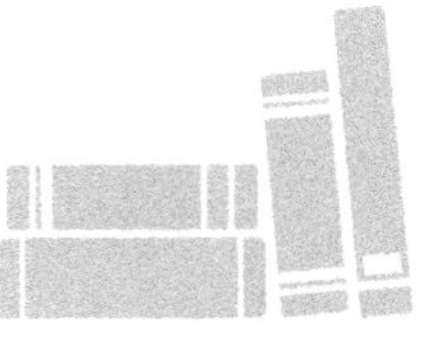

# BELOVED

## TEXTUAL ANALYSIS

## CHAPTER TWENTY-SEVEN: BARE FEET AND CHAMOMILE SAP

### STRUCTURE

Paul D's little ditty opens the chapter as a kind of summary of his relationship with Sethe. Clearly, he loves her and it is this love that will facilitate Sethe's healing process. Additionally, Morrison dates the novel again; it is now late summer.

### CHARACTERIZATION

At last, Paul D seems far less intimidated by his past or by a sense of powerlessness. Whatever has transpired in the months since his absence from 124 has made him a much steadier man. With Stamp Paid, he is able to laugh again. He accepts Denver as a grownup and reconciles with Sethe.

Out of his mouth, too, comes the important message of the novel: Sethe is her own "best thing." Paul D has grown. In accepting his past, he is able to face the future.

Also experiencing a great deal of growth is Denver. We see her in the world working, making friends, taking responsibility for her mother. This is not the same person who, at the beginning of the novel, was overcome by loneliness and an internal struggle over her mother's decision to commit infanticide.

Finally, there is Sethe, who still has no plans. Wounded, she is at a crossroads. She can resign from life, in much the same way Baby Suggs took to her bed to ponder color, or she can embrace it-establish a relationship with Paul D and accept herself as her own best thing. The novel's resolution comes out of her decision to try Paul D's way.

## THEME

The most important statement of the novel comes at its end. For so long Sethe has believed her children were her best things, that all-encompassing love was justification enough for her to kill rather than see them return to slavery. Morrison's truth, however, is that Sethe is her own best thing. And by extension, we are all our own best things.

## REALISM

More realistic detail comes in an examination of the black man's role in the Civil War. Black soldiers fought on both sides-185,000 in the Union Army alone. Promised equality, they were refused the same pay as white soldiers. It is true that Massachusetts eventually passed a law establishing such equity and that the state's black regiments, fighting for a cause, refused to accept the money.

Morrison also captures the magic of a slave's first free moments. Freedom meant many things. If you were black and in the south at the end of the war it meant facing a backlash of violence and exploitation. It also meant working, eating, sleeping, and loving whenever the feeling hit. Paul D learns this, along with the joy of making and spending his own money.

## SYMBOLISM

Here Boy's return, like his departure, is an omen. The sense of something "other"-the unexplainable-adds to Morrison's depiction of the supernatural.

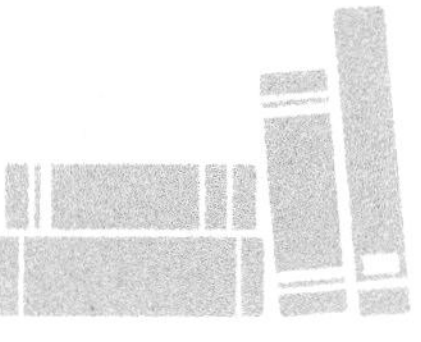

# BELOVED

## TEXTUAL ANALYSIS

## CHAPTER TWENTY-EIGHT: THERE IS A LONELINESS ...

### STRUCTURE

In epilogue fashion, the novel draws to a close with Morrison echoing many of the **themes** and images that have added depth to the story. Beloved is forgotten by a family and a community that deemed "remembering unwise." In characteristic fashion, repetition is used to emphasize the point: "This is not a story to pass on," and it isn't. The anguish that fed the act, the turmoil that it created in all the principals, has already been vanquished. It is time to face the future.

### THEME

Redemption comes as a result of reconciliation with the past. Morrison's characters are able to forget because they have lived through the pain of remembering. Thus, memory functions as catharsis.

## IRONY

Morrison's insistence that this is not a story to pass on is ironic in the sense that she has spent the last 275 pages doing just that-passing on this story to others.

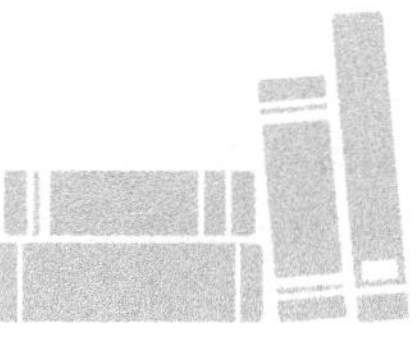

# BELOVED

## CHARACTER ANALYSES

### Beloved

There is very little to know about Beloved. A woman, about 19 or 20 years old, steps out of the water with new hands and feet and no memory of her past or present. On the one hand, she is a reincarnation of the daughter Sethe murdered 18 years before, and on the other, a representative voice of the 60 million or so Africans that were lost during the middle passage. But who is Beloved? Petulant and demanding, she seduces Paul D, captivates Denver, and almost destroys Sethe in a deadly game of domination. In her extended stay at 124, it is hard to pinpoint the aspects of character that would help define who she is. Beloved is more a presence, the intensity of which is determined by those who need her-for whatever reason-and are not afraid to call.

### Mr. Bodwin

As a white man and abolitionist, Bodwin represents a rare example of kindness to a black community habitually distrustful of whites. Born into privilege, he takes away from his childhood an abiding sense that all human life is sacred. The happiest years of his life, despite the ridicule, are spent in the struggle for abolition. In pursuit of that end, and out of a deep compassion for Sethe, he turns her one act of infanticide into a compelling argument against slavery and wins her release from jail. Over 70-his hopes for a tranquil republic dashed-he has begun to contemplate his own mortality and his desire is simple: to be allowed the pleasure of just one more day. Still, he remains generous as evidenced in his decision not to press charges against Sethe.

### Miss Bodwin

Bodwin's sister is also a fierce abolitionist. Denver remembers her as the kindly white woman who came to 124 at Christmas bearing gifts when Baby Suggs was alive. At the time, articulate on abolition matters and the Civil War, now she contents herself with "experimenting" on Denver, educating her in the hope she may one day go to Oberlin.

### Ella

In many respects, Ella represents community. Of course, she has her own story to tell. Everything is measured against "the lowest yet," a reference to her sexual captivity at the hands of a father and son. She is practical and unsentimental. Her advice to Sethe, "Don't love nothing," is telling because it is so basic. Her principles, her sense of right and wrong often make her high-minded and judgmental. She does not like prideful people and could not countenance Sethe after her release from prison. Yet, her turnabout with regard to Sethe suggests a softer side of her.

It is she who organizes the group of women who pray for Sethe. It is she who leads them, and it is she who ultimately stops Sethe from killing Bodwin. A strong and compassionate woman, she mirrors some of the best and worst qualities of the community.

### Garner, Paul A and Paul F.

As their names suggest, Paul A and Paul F-both brothers of Paul D-are indistinct. Paul F is sold by Mrs. Garner after Mr. Garner's death in order to sustain Sweet Home, and Paul A's whereabouts are unknown.

### Garner, Paul D

The last of the Sweet Home men is a wandering soul who discovers love at 124. On the move for years in an attempt to ward off the effects of Sweet Home and Alfred, Georgia, he wrestles with a growing sense of powerlessness and inadequacy. "What makes a man?" is his all-important query. Using Sixo and Halle as comparisons, even equating himself with Sweet Home's tough barnyard rooster, Mister, he struggles to work through the trauma of his slavery past. At 124, his sense of powerlessness is exacerbated by Beloved, who drives him out of Sethe's bed and later seduces him. The revelation of Sethe's "too thick" love pushes him completely away, but he returns a steadier and more confident man, capable of nursing Sethe back to physical and mental health.

### Mr. Garner

As the owner of Sweet Home, Garner's brand of slavery is less exploitative than others. He is "man enough" to allow his slave-men to carry guns; open enough to listen to their advice; and interested enough in them to teach them how to count. He is an enigma to his neighbors who do not hold his philosophies, and his braggadocio often leads him into fisticuffs. Garner's slavery is a matter of ego, though. He does his slaves no favor by creating such a "cradle" and after his death, it splits beyond recognition.

## Mrs. Garner

The wife of Sweet Home's plantation owner is painted as a woman of substance who experiences a steady decline. Her role as homemaker includes cooking, washing, making candles, soap and cider, etc., and she works right alongside first Baby Suggs, and then Sethe. Her closeness to the latter is evidenced by the wedding present earrings; and her tearful response to the news that Sethe was suckled by the nephews shows compassion. Still, she is very much a part of the traditional cast of southern society in her insistence that Schoolteacher come and manage the farm because it is inappropriate for her to be the only white woman among so many male slaves.

## Lady Jones

The name Lady Jones tags an important characteristic about this educated, mulatto schoolteacher, and that is her separation-both real and imagined-from others in the community. As a "high yellow" black woman she fights hard for inclusion. She marries the "Blackest man" she can find, has "rainbow colored" children whom she educates along with the rest of the community's progeny, and sends them off to a black college. Yet, she feels unwanted and unloved. She befriends Denver as someone in need, but shows her disdain for the ignorance of superstition by refusing to accompany the townswomen in their efforts to help Sethe escape from the grasp of Beloved.

## Paid, Stamp

A prime example of the ancestor-elder in the novel, Stamp Paid is as good and decent man with a commitment to community that is unparalleled. Born Joshua, he changes his name to Stamp Paid rather than kill someone after his wife is forced to bed with the master's son. Then and there he assumes a debtlessness and spends his life helping others do the same-as an agent for the underground railroad, as a community leader, and a friend. His relationship with Baby Suggs, Denver, and Sethe is especially touching because it emphasizes his sense of caring and concern. His guilt over telling Paul D Sethe's secret is part of that. His principles keep him moving even though he is bone tired. Stamp Paid represents the best aspects of community.

## Sawyer

Sethe's restaurant boss is portrayed as a kindly man who takes a chance on hiring Sethe after her release from prison, but who becomes more and more irritated with the hired help after the death of his son in the Civil War.

## Schoolteacher

The brother-in-law of Mr. Garner, Schoolteacher arrives at the request of Mrs. Garner to set the Sweet Home Plantation straight. To know his name is to know him. More than just his profession, he is the embodiment of a strict formality and matter-of-factness one might expect from a schoolteacher. He walks around in a collar, even in the fields, pad and pen in hand, taking notes and making observations on the behavior of the slaves. His lesson plans include a comparison of the animal and human characteristics of the slaves. Schoolteacher represents many of the assumptions and prejudices created to justify slavery. He considers himself a superior man who must ultimately assume the responsibility of saving his slaves from "the cannibal life they preferred." He also believes that life is a series of lessons to be taught to others. One nephew stays behind in the search for Sethe in order to learn his-that you cannot mistreat "creatures" and expect them not to react.

## Sixo

A young man in his 20s when we first meet him, Sixo is, like Halle in Paul D's eyes, a sterling example of manhood. "Indigo with a flame-red tongue," he is closer to the African experience. He is a spirited and spiritual man who takes night walks and dances among the trees to keep his bloodlines open. He is also rebellious, clever, and persistent. He dies laughing, secure in the knowledge that his seed will live on. As a black man who is not afraid to fight back, he poses a serious threat to the institution of slavery.

## Suggs, Baby

Baby Suggs, Halle's mother and Sethe's mother-in-law, is one of the most important characters in the book, not only because she brings the lesson of self-love and self-possession to the community, but because of her role as ancestor-elder. Stoic and a realist in much the same way as Ella, she adapts to slavery and motherhood by learning not to love her children. With Halle, however, she feels free to invest that emotion and it is he who buys her freedom. Baby Suggs is a commanding woman. A great believer in the power of God, she leads the community in weekly celebrations of self. More than that she opens her home and her heart to anyone in need. She is devastated, however, by Sethe's impulse to kill and retires to her bed to ponder color. It is, for her, a way of giving up; everything she has attempted to do with her life is negated in that one instant. Even after her death, her presence pervades the novel and she becomes a tangible force in Denver's life by encouraging her to step beyond 124 to help save her mother.

## Suggs, Howard and Buglar

The young sons of Sethe and Halle run away from home after the ghost intimidates them with her spite.

## Suggs, Denver

Denver's growth-the degree to which she takes possession of herself-is an exciting prospect, given her early trauma. At 18, she leaves a world of painful isolation where she finds refuge in the secret world of the boxwood arbor and the friendship of the baby ghost. Her loneliness is exacerbated by the departure of her two brothers and the death of her grandmother. She longs for connections, some of which she finds in Sethe's stories of her birth. Still, she is traumatized as a result of Sethe's act of infanticide and struggles to work through the varied feelings she has toward her mother. Her dreams are nightmarish; she is afraid to let Sethe braid her hair; and she goes deaf because she cannot handle other people's questions about Sethe or stomach the answers herself. When she returns to the world of the hearing, she finds solace in the baby ghost and later in the arrival of Beloved as ghost incarnate. It is a friendship that grows dangerous very quickly because of its obsessional qualities. Just as Beloved wants to possess Sethe, so Denver wants to possess Beloved. She cultivates that relationship until she realizes the toll Beloved's presence has taken on Sethe. She moves to help her mother and in doing so reconciles whatever conflict existed between them.

### Suggs, Halle

As Sethe's husband and Baby Suggs' son, Halle's presence is a function of memory. Sethe remembers him as the loving husband who abandoned her. Paul D remembers him as the man who captured Sethe's heart, but lost his wits at the sight of his wife being suckled by a young white man. Baby Suggs remembers him as the one who gave her freedom. Halle is a good man, honorable because he buys his mother out of slavery, and considers buying his family out as well before he considers running; and ambitious because he is willing to learn whatever Mr. Garner has to teach. In Paul D's eyes, he is a man's man.

### Suggs, Sethe

Sethe is, perhaps, the most complexly rendered character. It is her story that informs the novel. Raised in the "cradle" of Sweet Home, she is unrealistic in her expectations of what slavery will allow her as a person and a mother. She invests so much in both, but most especially motherhood, because she believes her children are her "best things." Her decision to seek freedom is, in part, due to her desire that they have a different life from the one she has known. Schoolteacher's arrival to take them back sends her reeling and she takes what she deems as appropriate action; she tries to kill her children. Succeeding with one, she lives for 18 years with her guilt and with the almost daily tyranny of the baby ghost. Sethe handles it, accepting its presence as a reminder of the child that died and as a manifestation of her own guilt. So closely is she locked into the cycle of guilt and remorse that when Paul D exorcises the familiar, she calls it back. Beloved's arrival and Sethe's gradual discovery of who she is cements the process of decline. After Paul D's absence, she surrenders and the two become entangled in a parasitic relationship that almost claims Sethe's life. Sethe's rescue at the hands of the community, and her reconciliation with Paul D, signal an end to the cycle of destruction. She must learn to accept herself as her own "best thing."

## 30 Mile Woman

Although she appears in the book briefly and only in the context of memory, the 30 Mile Woman is a symbol of Sixo's rebellion. He leaves Sweet Home at night to meet her; they plan to run together; she is pregnant with his child. As Sixo puts it, "She gather me, man. The pieces I am, she gather them and give them back to me in all the right order."

## Wagon, Janey

Janey Wagon, as housekeeper to the Bodwins since her early adolescence, functions as another voice of the community. A gossip, she is curious, concerned, and judgmental about Sethe's visitation from Beloved. Yet, she is also the first to articulate that Beloved's presence is no accident, and her quick move to spread the word is a major factor in Sethe's rescue.

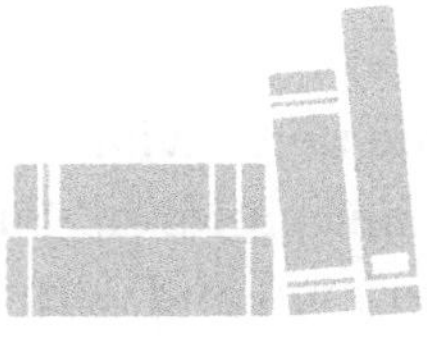

# BELOVED

## GUIDE TO FURTHER STUDY

### IDEAS FOR PAPERS, ORAL REPORTS, AND DISCUSSION

1. Compare and contrast the generational conflicts that exist for the women who inhabit 124.

2. How is the **theme** of the pariah manifested in the novel?

3. Compare and contrast the images of women-both black and white.

4. Assess the mythic structure of the novel. Consider, for example, aspects of quest, renunciation, and redemption.

5. Outline the course of Denver's development from child to woman.

6. What is the effect of gradually revealing Sethe's past, and how does this method relate to the **themes** in the book?

7. Compare the relationship between Denver and Beloved, and Beloved and Sethe.

8. What are the advantages or effects of using memory as a means of **exposition** and characterization?

9. Discuss the significance of Sethe's slavery experience in her decision to commit infanticide. How does her experience differ from Paul D's? Give examples.

10. What function does Mrs. Garner serve in the novel?

11. Morrison has commented that the novel deals with "certain aspects of self-sabotage." What does she mean?

12. In what way is *Beloved* a "tragedy"? What is Sethe's "tragic flaw"?

13. Discuss briefly Sethe's comment, "No more running from nothing. I will never run from another thing on this earth."

14. Why is Paul D's sense of powerlessness emphasized so much throughout the novel?

15. Water, especially as it relates to *Beloved,* is used as a symbol-motif of birth, death, and rebirth. In what ways is this motif applicable to other characters and events in the novel.?

16. Relate the epigraph to the development of **theme** in the novel.

17. How is nature used in *Beloved*?

18. What is the function of the minor characters?

19. In what respect are all the major characters victims?

20. Why does Sethe call Beloved back once Paul D has exorcised the baby ghost?

21. How does Morrison arouse and sustain our interest in Sixo?

22. Discuss Paul D's reconciliation with Sethe. Is it believable? Why or why not?

23. Discuss the tensions underlying Denver and Sethe's relationship. How are they finally resolved?

24. Discuss the role of religion in the novel.

25. In what ways is the setting important to the **theme** of *Beloved*?

26. Discuss Morrison's use of the first person narrator in the context of the entire novel.

27. What happens to Beloved at the end of the novel? Has she really been vanquished?

28. How does Morrison contrast Ella and Sethe?

29. Discuss Morrison's treatment of whites.

30. What is the principal device the characters use to handle their suffering?

31. Is Beloved a villain? Explain.

32. How does Morrison develop a sense of continuity between the past and the present?

33. Discuss the dual roles of community. How are they manifested in *Beloved*?

34. What is the principal lesson of the novel and how is it reinforced?

35. How does each character's reaction to the past and the present affect his or her characterization?

36. In what respect is Paul D the hero of the novel?

37. Compare and contrast Ella and Stamp Paid.

38. What larger significance does "pondering color" have?

39. Discuss Morrison's identification of black women as stoic figures.

40. What is the significance of "plans"? Why don't Sethe and Paul D ever make any?

41. Who or what is Beloved? What evidence do we have to suggest that she is something other than Sethe's dead daughter returned from the grave?

42. Discuss the issue of identity as it relates to the major characters.

43. How does Morrison use the story of Lot's wife and the image of the Medusa to characterize Beloved?

44. Discuss the uses of **irony** in the book.

45. Read several reviews of *Beloved* (see Bibliography) and report on the main criticisms, negative and positive.

46. Compare and contrast *Beloved* with an earlier novel by Morrison. Consider themes, plot, point-of-view, tone, methods of narration and of characterization.

47. Read Morrison's article "Rediscovering Black History" (see Bibliography). In what ways can you see here the beginnings of her work on *Beloved*?

48. Read *The Black Book*, an anthology edited by Morrison, with special attention to the article "A Visit to the Slave Mother Who Killed Her Child." Show how Morrison developed this article into the novel *Beloved*. How much of *Beloved* is based on the article; how much is fictitious expansion of the original story?

49. Read several interviews of Morrison in which she discusses *Beloved*. What were her aims in writing the novel? What methods did she consciously employ?

50. In a dictionary or handbook of psychological terms, read the entry on stream-of-consciousness. Read a portion of James Joyce's Ulysses and compare his use of the "stream" with Morrison's in *Beloved*.

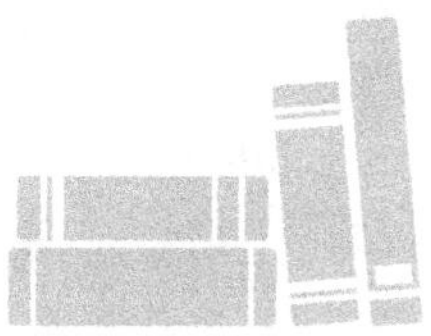

# BIBLIOGRAPHY

## WORKS BY TONI MORRISON

*The Bluest Eye*. New York: Holt, Rinehart & Winston, Inc., 1970.

*Sula*. New York: Alfred A. Knopf, 1973.

*Song of Solomon*. New York: Alfred A. Knopf, 1977.

*Tar Baby*. New York: Alfred A. Knopf, 1981.

*Beloved*. New York: Alfred A. Knopf, 1987.

Morrison, Toni, "Rootedness: The Ancestor As Foundation," Mari Evans, ed., *Black Women Writers* (1950–1980): A Critical Evaluation, New York: Anchor Press/Doubleday, 1984, pp. 339–345. Morrison addresses the particular concerns she brings to her writing.

____. "Rediscovering Black History," *New York Times Magazine* (August 11, 1974), pp. 14–16, 18, 20, 22, 24. Morrison recounts her experience as editor of The Black Book. One article from the work, "A Visit to the Slave Mother Who Killed Her Child," was inspiration for *Beloved*.

____. "A Slow Walk of Trees," *New York Times Magazine* (July 4, 1976), pp. 104, 150, 152, 156, 160, 162, 164. A personal assessment of the progress black people made from post-Civil War America to the 1970s.

## WRITINGS ABOUT MORRISON AND HER WORKS

Atwood, Margaret, "Haunted by Their Nightmares," *New York Times Book Review* (September 13, 1987), pp. 1, 49–50. Review compliments Morrison's use of language and her presentation of the supernatural.

Baker-Fletcher, Karen, "Fierce Love Comes to Haunt," *Commonweal*, Vol. 114 (November 6, 1987), pp. 631–633. Raises questions on the nature of Sethe's crime and beyond that, why the novel was written.

Bakerman, Jane, "The Seams Can't Show: An Interview with Toni Morrison," *Black American Literature Forum*, Vol. 12 (Summer 1978), pp. 56–60. Morrison expounds upon her own writing.

Brown, Rosellen, "The Pleasure of Enchantment," *Nation*, Vol. 245 (October 17, 1987), pp. 418–421. Complimentary review acknowledges visual appeal of the book but questions its resolution as being too hastily achieved.

Clemons, Walter, "The Ghosts of 'Sixty Million and More,'" *Newsweek*, Vol. 110 (September 28, 1987), p. 75. Short discussion of the book's dedication, including an interview with Morrison.

____. "A Gravestone of Memories," *Newsweek*, Vol. 110 (September 28, 1987), pp. 74–75. Review analyzes juxtaposition of ghost story against backdrop of black life in post-war Cincinnati.

Crouch, Stanley, "Aunt Medea," *The New Republic*, Vol. 194 (October 19, 1987), pp. 38–43. Analysis of the novel in the context of black literary criticism a la James Baldwin. Crouch considers the book melodramatic and "protest pulp fiction."

Davis, Hope Hale, "Casting a Strong Spell," *New Leader*, Vol. 70 (November 2, 1987), pp. 20–21. Review of the novel and overview of Morrison's other works.

Dowling, Colette, "The Song of Toni Morrison," *New York Times Magazine* (May 20, 1979), pp. 40–2, 48, 52, 54, 56, 58. Comprehensive interview with the author covering her life and times.

Edwards, Thomas R., "Ghost Story," *New York Review of Books*, Vol. 34 (November 5, 1987), pp. 18–19. Exploration of novel that champions language, fusion of myth and fantasy, Morrison's compassion and ability to capture the injustices of slavery and their impact on slaves and former slaves.

Fikes, Robert, Jr., "Echoes from Small Town Ohio: A Toni Morrison Bibliography," *Obsidian: Black Literature in Review*, Vol. I/II (Spring/Summer 1979), pp. 142–148. Older bibliography of works by and about Morrison and her published writings.

Gray, Paul, "Something Terrible Happened," *Time* Vol. 130 (September 21, 1987), p. 75. Review suggests Morrison's treatment of slavery is both "intriguing" and "unsettling."

Horn, Miriam, "'Five Years of Terror,'" *U.S. News & World Report*, Vol. 103 (October 19, 1987), p. 75. Morrison speaks out on racism.

Iannone, Carol, "Toni Morrison's Career," *Commentary*, Vol. 84 (December 1987), pp. 59–63. Brief biographical account of Morrison's life and examination of her novels including a review of *Beloved*. Iannone argues the dimensions of tragedy in the novel are overdone.

LeClair, Thomas, "The Language Must Not Sweat," *New Republic*, Vol. 184 (March 21, 1981), pp. 25–29. Question and answer interview with Morrison in which she talks about her life, her work, and her writing. "What is hard for me is to be simple, to have uncomplex stories with complex people in them, to clean the language, really clean it."

Rothstein, Mervyn, "Toni Morrison, In Her New Novel Defends Women," *New York Times* (August 26, 1987), p. C17(L). Morrison talks about writing *Beloved*.

Smith, Amanda, "Toni Morrison," *Publishers Weekly*, Vol. 232 (August 21, 1987), pp. 50–51. Interview and review that discuss impetus behind *Beloved*, the real-life story of the former slave woman who tried to murder her children when caught by her former master.

Strouse, Jean, "Toni Morrison's Black Magic," *Newsweek*, Vol. 97 (March 30, 1981), pp. 52–57. In-depth interview with Morrison that examines her background, her novels, and her literary philosophies.

Tate, Claudia, "Introduction," Claudia Tate, ed., *Black Women Writers at Work*, New York: Continuum, 1983, pp. XV–XXVI. Offers a discussion of thematic concerns of black women writers.

_____. "Toni Morrison," Claudia Tate, ed., *Black Women Writers at Work*, New York: Continuum, 1983, pp. 117–131. Wide-ranging interview with Morrison on issues ranging from success to community.

Thurman, Judith, "A House Divided," *New Yorker* Vol. 63 (November 2, 1987), pp. 175–180. Review points out some excesses, "a chorus of stock characters" and "prose rife with motifs and images that the narration sometimes orchestrates too solemnly."

Washington, Mary H., "Introduction," Mary Helen Washington, ed., *Black-Eyed Susans*, New York: Anchor Press/Doubleday, 1975. Interesting and insightful discussion on **themes** in the literature of black women.

CPSIA information can be obtained
at www.ICGtesting.com
Printed in the USA
BVHW042108030820
585401BV00015B/460